The ROI Mindset *is a compr* *necessary to succeed in organi* *to digest complex fundraisin* *organization's development strategy, and critical markers for appropriate execution. A unique component of* The ROI Mindset *is that it tackles the natural anxiety novice and experienced development professionals have when asking for financial support. These skills are not usually taught in a classroom but must be acquired as you acclimate to the profession. Joanne Oppelt provides key tactics upfront that often aren't achieved until a few years in the field.*

Dominic Prophete, JD
Chief Executive Officer
Wynona's House Child Advocacy Center

As a first time Executive Director, I was looking for a resource that would have it all. This book is it! I learned so much from the real-world case studies. I felt that I was reading about my own experiences every chapter! I highly recommend it for any nonprofit executive looking to take their nonprofit to the next level.

Sara Huisking, MBA, CFRE
Executive Director
Sound Start Foundation

Are you tired of people expecting you to do more with less? Do you long to have more money to invest in advancing your mission? I've been in your shoes and involved with nonprofits for over 40 years. This book is different from other fundraising books you've seen or read. Does the idea of having continuous net surpluses excite you? Or are you thinking: "Is she crazy?" No! I'm not. This book is the answer. It gives you a roadmap and empowers you with the "how tos" you need to create a fundraising system that yields those net surpluses. Implement what it teaches you and you will get results.

Mary Hiland, PhD
President
Hiland Consulting

If you're looking for a mentor to help you hone essential skills on your nonprofit journey, read Joanne Oppelt. You'd be hard-pressed to find a better blueprint for success—whether you seek transition from line-staff to supervisor, supervisor to manager, or manager to visionary leader.

Steven L Meyers, PhD
Founder and Chief Executive Officer
Personalized Philanthropy: Advising and Coaching Non-Profits and Donors

Every time I hear a nonprofit say things like, "We're the best kept secret in town," "How come XYZ organization always get great media coverage, can recruit top-notch board members, and gets so much funding, while our nonprofit struggles to just get by?" or "We just need to go out and find new donors—help!" I will refer them to this book. Joanne covers the importance of collaboration instead of competition, both internally and in the community; helps nonprofits get out of the scarcity mentality that is so prevalent among them; and teaches them how to not scare away good board members with aggressive fundraising expectations. Her real-life examples of nonprofit leaders who made this system work will help the reader create a plan for their success.

Linda Lysakowski, ACFRE
Nonprofit Management and Fundraising Consultant
Linda Lysakowski Consulting

THE ROI MINDSET
How to Raise More Money With the Budget You Have

THE ROI MINDSET
How to Raise More Money With the Budget You Have

JOANNE OPPELT, MHA, CNC, CDE, CNE

The ROI Mindset: How to Raise More Money with the Budget You Have

Published by Joanne Oppelt Consulting, LLC

Copyright © 2022 by Joanne Oppelt

Hardcover ISBN: 978-1-951978-27-3
Paperback ISBN: 978-1-951978-26-6
eBook ISBN: 978-1-951978-28-0

13 12 11 10 9 8 7 6 5 4 3 2 1

Printed in the United States of America

Dedication

This book is dedicated to all the executive directors who give their blood, sweat, and tears to moving their nonprofits forward.

Table of Contents

About the Author

Joanne Oppelt, MHA, CNC, CDE, CNE

During Joanne Oppelt's 30+ years working in the nonprofit arena, she has held positions from volunteer to executive director in both small and large organizations. Integrating fundraising with strategic planning, marketing, operations, and financial systems, she builds up organizational revenue streams, creating sustainable funding structures. Her extensive background puts her in a unique position to understand the challenges nonprofit leaders face—both internally and externally. As principal of Joanne Oppelt Consulting, LLC, she specializes in helping nonprofits improve their ROI and realize continuous net surpluses. She currently provides consulting services, multi-module online courses with private coaching, person-to-person fundraising advice, annual summits, virtual get-togethers, and weekly newsletters.

The creator of The Sustainable High ROI Fundraising System and co-creator of the Nonprofit Quick Guide series, Joanne is the author of six books and coauthor of fourteen. She has taught at Kean University and is a highly sought-after speaker and presenter. She holds a master's degree in health administration and a bachelor's degree in education, with a minor in psychology.

She can be reached at joanne@joanneoppelt.com or through her website www.joanneoppeltcourses.com.

Acknowledgements

As always, I give thanks to my husband, Rick, who encourages me to continue to ply my craft despite the hours it takes me. It is my hope that you feel as supported by me as I do you.

And to my friends and colleagues—Mary Hiland, Ph.D. and Sara Huisking, M.B.A., CFRE—who reviewed the manuscript in its draft stage. Your feedback made this a better book.

Mary—your friendship, support, thoroughness, and analytical mind help me tremendously. I appreciate your perspective as a former executive director from the program side of things. You make me connect the dots that are second nature to me. You ensure I clearly explain how to implement my system to those who may not have had much exposure to the fundraising field. And your patience is remarkable. I appreciate our personal and professional relationship more than words can express.

Sara—we have much in common. As a first-time executive director, it is wonderful to see you blossom into your role and manage it with aplomb. I am lucky to work with you. I admire you greatly.

I also want to thank Palmetto Publishing for designing, editing, and laying out this book. Jack and Katie, your team is tops!

Thank you all! It truly does take a village.

Chapter One

Besieged

Julia tried to calm the butterflies in her stomach. The community theater she led had not met their third quarter fundraising goals. She was meeting with her finance committee later that afternoon and shuddered as she thought about how the year-to-date deficit was going to be received. She anticipated a tense meeting.

They would just have to make up the deficit from their year-end fundraising activities. If all went well, she reasoned, they would make up the difference and enter the new year in a stable financial position. Perhaps, if her board and staff worked really hard and were extremely successful, they could replace part of the thirty days of operating reserves they had tapped into to get through the summer. After all, they still had time to pump up their gala attendance, Giving Tuesday campaign, and holiday appeal.

She adjusted her revenue projections to reflect her hopes for the fourth quarter. She would ask her finance committee members to push other board members to sell more gala tickets and ask more of their friends and business colleagues to donate to the holiday appeal.

And her development director would just have to work harder to find new donors. New donors were out there. It was just a matter of spreading the word about the good work her organization does more broadly. The community should respond positively. She hoped.

What This Book is About

Have you ever been in a situation like Julia's, where your fundraising is not going as planned, the pressure is building, and you try to bring all-hands-on-deck to help you reach your financial goals? Where you double down on your fundraising efforts to meet your budget objectives? Where it's crucial that you bring in money because your reserves are dwindling? Where there is no other alternative than raise as much money as possible?

Of course, you have. As executive directors, we've all been there.

This book gives you a roadmap to moving from pressure-filled situations like Julia's to much more pleasant experiences of realizing net surpluses. This book doesn't tell you the tasks involved in implementing any one fundraising activity. It does, however, tell you how to implement a fundraising system that increases net revenues and is sustainable over time.

What Makes This Book Different

Usually, fundraising books are about the mechanics of implementing specific fundraising pursuits, for example, writing appeal letters, asking for major gifts, writing grants, running capital campaigns, asking your board to fundraise, and the like. This book is different. This book will tell you how to build the infrastructure you need to raise the serious amounts of money you desire.

This book is written for executive directors who want to raise more money to advance their nonprofits' missions. Based on my more than thirty years

> ### Clarifying Point
>
> This book is not about the mechanics of conducting different fundraising activities. Rather, this book is a guide for implementing your own Sustainable High ROI Fundraising System so that you can realize remarkably more fundraising net income than you currently are

of non-profit experience, this book teaches you how to implement a fundraising system resulting in sustainable revenue streams that produces a high return on investment (ROI) in terms of both money *and* mission. It relies on proven fundraising fundamentals, best practices in the field, and principles of organizational leadership and growth. How I apply these concepts to attain a sustainably high ROI fundraising system through a robust development team is what makes this book unique.

So that you can see how the system is implemented in real life, I provide you candid examples of how it was applied at various nonprofits. Just so you know, since the examples are real, some of the details have been changed to protect confidentiality.

What This Book Covers

Chapters Two through Five outline the principles of building and operating a sustainable fundraising system that produces both high mission and financial returns. **Chapter Two** reintroduces you to The Sustainable High ROI Fundraising System, which I explain at length in my companion book *The Sustainable High ROI Fundraising System*, and the power the system unleashes when implemented properly.

Chapter Three covers how to create the fundraising efficiencies critical to setting your development staff up for success. We move on to talk about the mindset you need to successfully implement The Sustainable High ROI Fundraising System in **Chapter Four**. I define scarcity and abundance mentalities, the effects of mindset on meeting your fundraising goals, and how to overcome a debilitating outlook. **Chapter Five** explores six keys to successfully working with your whole team—board, staff, and volunteers—when raising money: shared and servant leadership, teamwork, goal setting, planning, evaluation, and mitigating risk.

Chapters Six and Seven focus on developing the infrastructure you need to realize net surpluses. In **Chapter Six**, we talk about how to fund building your organizational capacity when money is scarce, as is the case for most nonprofits. **Chapter Seven** explains how to efficiently collect and record the data you need to effectively evaluate your financial and marketing performance.

Chapters Eight and Nine cover the process of asking for money, the driver of The Sustainable High ROI Fundraising System. **Chapter Eight** describes how to get comfortable talking about money with donors, techniques for overcoming fears about asking, and how to look calm when you are stressed. **Chapter Nine** goes into all things asking, including asking techniques that guarantee a positive reception, how to make the ask itself, overcoming common giving concerns, and how the executive director and development director work together to get the gift.

Chapter Ten shows you how to build a supportive community and invite donors into your nonprofit family. We cover how to identify key stakeholders and create messages that will wow them. We also talk about attracting new donors by identifying, engaging, recruiting, and asking them. And how you can be efficient in all these efforts.

Next, we turn our attention toward the human component of the system: the cadre of board members, staff, and volunteers you work with. **Chapter Eleven** delineates your fundraising dream team of board, staff, and volunteers. We also speak to affording talent on a shoestring budget. **Chapter Twelve** talks about how to recruit good board members, development professionals, and fundraising volunteers, including how to find them and interview questions to ask them.

Chapter Thirteen speaks to retaining the team you've built and gives you actionable suggestions for enticing valuable team members to stay. **Chapter Fourteen** focuses on the need for continuing professional development, its cost-effectiveness, and how to make sure there is money for it.

When you implement a new system, you are changing the status quo. And that's not an easy task. **Chapter Fifteen** delves into effecting change. We talk about two different models for implementing change, their pros and cons, and how to approach their unexpected consequences.

We wrap up our discussion in **Chapter Sixteen** with a review of the tools and processes critical to successfully implementing The Sustainable High ROI Fundraising System.

By the end of this book, you will be able to:

- Apply the four essential precepts outlined in *The Sustainable High ROI Fundraising System* to successfully achieve fundraising growth.

- Fund the infrastructure you need to move forward.

- Recruit and retain the board members, development professionals, and volunteers who make up your fundraising team.

- Plan and set expectations regarding the changes you want to make.

- Achieve continuous net surpluses to sustainably build your organization's capacity and advance your nonprofit's mission.

The Author's Underlying Beliefs

I believe the ultimate goal of leading your nonprofit forward is to forever change the human condition, making the world a better place to live. And I believe passion is not enough. Meeting mission takes money.

I believe that fundraising, just like mission fulfillment, is an organizational effort. Which means that everyone involved in your agency contributes to raising money in one way or another. For example, how your receptionist answers the phone effects how the caller, a member of the community, perceives your organization. How well your IT specialist protects your electronic data determines how much trust donors have in your ability to protect their confidential information. What individual staff members communicate to their friends, who are community members, about their work experiences influences word-of-mouth publicity about your organization. Every facet of your operations affects your nonprofit's ability to raise money in one way or another.

Which means that fundraising is not just about raising money. It's about implementing organization-wide enhancements and creating a culture of philanthropy.

Shifting Mindset

Think of fundraising not as a series of transactions about money, but as a tool to infuse healthy attitudes about raising money into the essence of your nonprofit and launch a culture of philanthropy into your community.

It is my intention that, through this book, I not only help you raise more money to advance your mission, but that I also help you begin to change your organizational culture. Because sustainability is not only about the dollars and cents. Sustainability is about continuous growth in terms of both money *and* mission. You need both. And you need both to feed off of one another. Your objective is to have enough money to meet more mission then use the fact you meet more mission to raise more money. Which, in turn, funds meeting even more mission. This cycle is how nonprofits change the world. My goal is to give you the tools to build it.

You have a formidable job. It's not for the faint of heart. Changing the world is hard work. But you can do it! I believe in you. I believe you got to where you are because you have what it takes. Let's take the next step in your fundraising journey together.

Julia's Solution

Julia's situation did change. The community theater did eventually realize a surplus. But first Julia had to stop and look at her fundraising system as a whole rather than as a series of activities. She needed to move her board to focus on governance and income generation strategy instead of pulling them into fundraising operations. She needed to realize more net income without incurring added costs. She needed to excite her community so that potential donors became involved with her agency. And she needed a way to fund her growing outreach efforts.

As Julia implemented The Sustainable High ROI Fundraising System, she built a strong fundraising infrastructure. As a result, board members, staff, and volunteers raised more money at less cost. She and her board infused a culture of philanthropy into the nonprofit and her organization became more well-known and resourced. Using The

Sustainable High ROI System framework, Julia was able to grow her agency and advance her mission in ways she had only dreamed of before.

Wrapping It Up

You, too, can realize positive results. Although your situation may be different than Julia's, the principles and techniques I describe in this book apply. You can go from stressed and not meeting fundraising goals to calm, knowing you will have a net surplus. You won't be going from fundraising activity to fundraising activity hoping something works. You will have the infrastructure and organizational capacity you need to grow. And you will have a proven system—The Sustainable High ROI Fundraising System—to direct you.

Points to Remember

- This book teaches you how to implement a fundraising system resulting in sustainable revenue streams that produce a high return on investment in terms of both money and mission.

- You can change your fundraising situation. Not by working harder at executing specific fundraising activities, but by creating a strong infrastructure that builds your organizational capacity.

- By the end of this book, you will have the tools you need to meet your financial goals, recruit and retain a strong fundraising team, navigate the challenges that are part of the change process, and achieve the net surpluses you need to sustainably advance your nonprofit's mission.

What's Next

The next chapter reintroduces the components of The Sustainable High ROI Fundraising System and the results you can achieve by putting each component into operation. The rest of the book focuses on the infrastructure you need to successfully implement the system at your nonprofit.

Chapter Two

The Sustainable High ROI Fundraising System

The mission of the small international aid agency Courtney leads is to alleviate poverty through microenterprise, specifically by providing funding for basic needs and the start-up of family-owned businesses in Guatemala and Nigeria. She and her board wanted to acquire younger donors to increase fundraising revenues.

Its donor base was pretty loyal, evident through a high overall donor retention rate. One hundred percent of its board gave an annual major gift. Many of its donors were also major givers. The problem was that as its older donors retired, moved away, or passed on, the nonprofit had not been able to replace them. Its donor base was shrinking, and as a result, revenues were declining. No matter what she did, Courtney just couldn't attract younger donors. She was at a loss as to what to do.

The Sustainable High ROI Fundraising System

The Sustainable High ROI Fundraising System teaches you how to empower your board members to become mission leaders, facilitate fundraising staff success, and lead your community to support your agency. Implementing the system allows you to raise more money with less effort, increasing your return on investment—your investment being time and money.

The system looks like this:

There are four key factors that make the system unique:

1. I emphasize advancing mission just as much as raising money, so you build on your board's motivation for serving and increase your nonprofit's appeal to potential donors.

2. I don't just focus on raising revenues but also on ensuring your expenses are kept to a minimum, so you increase your return on investment.

3. I take a strategic approach that mobilizes all your stakeholders—your board, staff *and* community.

4. I help you create a culture shift within your nonprofit, so board members and staff become consistent mission ambassadors for your organization.

Assessing Your Fundraising Strengths and Gaps

Step one of The Sustainable High ROI Fundraising System involves assessing the efficiency and effectiveness of your agency's fundraising strategy and use of organizational mission and financial assets. It uses a strengths-based approach. You use the system as a basis for choosing methods of raising money that will work within the parameters of your nonprofit's capacity, while at the same time growing it. As a result, you create a customized action plan that moves your fundraising forward and establishes benchmarks for measuring your progress.

Results you can expect after implementing this step:

- A financial strategy that leverages your agency's fundraising assets and works within your organization's capacity

- An action plan that shows you how to take the next step toward financial stability and mission impact

- Improvement in your fundraising return on investment by at least 100 percent

Empowering Your Board

Step two of the system is empowering your board to fundraise. Your board is the most valuable leadership asset your nonprofit has. Board members teach the community how to interact with your agency. The board is where an infectious fundraising culture starts. During step two, you help your board become comfortable with fundraising. You help them develop skills so that they become strong and consistent mission ambassadors. You then build on their efforts to leverage existing organizational resources.

Results you can expect after implementing this step are:

- Board members who promote your nonprofit to the community

- A leadership culture that enables you and your staff to capitalize on your nonprofit's fundraising assets and the strong community support board members have created

- Board and staff leaders who work together in a supportive relationship for fundraising

Mobilizing Your Staff

Step three of the system mobilizes your staff. To ensure your staff achieves success, you create an environment conducive to fundraising and give your staff the tools necessary to meet the financial and mission goals you and the board have set. This step focuses on how you can leverage the never-enough resources available to you to reach those goals. You want to spread mission while realizing the best possible returns on your investments of time and money.

To implement the system efficiently, you work with the staff and board concurrently. Together, they spread your nonprofit's message, advancing its mission.

Results you can expect after implementing this step:

- More donors

- Higher donations

- Reduced fundraising costs

- A development work plan that encompasses total fundraising operations, including technology, communications, campaigns and appeals, staffing, and board involvement

Exciting Your Community

Most fundraising interventions miss the critical step of exciting the community and why it's essential. In this step, you capitalize on and influence community perceptions of your nonprofit so that you attract more community financial and mission backing.

You prepare to excite your community as you mobilize your staff and engage your board in fundraising. You want the infectious fundraising culture you and the board have created to infiltrate your community. Your goal is to raise your nonprofit's profile to draw people to your cause and financially support your agency.

Results you can expect after implementing this step:

- More awareness of your nonprofit in the community

- Unified, consistent messaging that rallies the public to support your mission

- More advocates for your cause

- Increased financial support

The Ultimate Outcome

Using The Sustainable High ROI Fundraising System results in more financial reserves, money to improve infrastructure, funds to build long-term financial assets that solidify your nonprofit's financial position, and money to grow your nonprofit's impact and advance its mission. By implementing this system, you realize the resource efficiencies it offers, raising more money at less cost. For a thorough and complete discussion of this system, I recommend reading my companion book *The Sustainable High ROI Fundraising System.*

Implementing the System

Of course, knowing the system is one thing. Implementing it is another. Systems interventions affect the whole agency and require coordination organization wide. Most nonprofits have a structure within which each department and the board work are engaged with the mission but not very closely with each other.

Typical Nonprofit Fundraising System Relationships

The goal of The Sustainable High ROI Fundraising System is to more closely integrate departments and functions, adopting an infrastructure that weaves fundraising into the fabric of your nonprofit and where almost all organizational resources are devoted to mission fulfillment. What you end up with looks more like the diagram below, where departments are not only coordinating activities but working together as one big team to reach the common goals of mission and financial sustainability.

Mission and Financial Sustainability

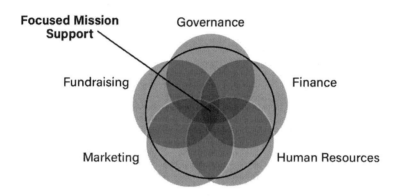

Case Study: How the System Worked

Courtney was my point of contact at the small international aid agency wanting to attract younger donors. I gave her a questionnaire, including questions about mission and mission growth, board leadership and structure, financial health and performance, fundraising infrastructure, marketing and communications endeavors, and volunteer recruitment, training, and development systems. She completed the form in partnership with her executive committee. I received the information, analyzed the data, and reported back to her. She took the information to her whole board where they voted to move forward with our engagement. Courtney and I then went to work.

What was notable about this nonprofit was the depth of the relationships with community government and leadership. This was a strength we definitely wanted to build on in recruiting new donors. They also had a basic donation infrastructure, including having defined major gift levels and corresponding materials. The existing volunteer structure was robust and worked well for them. We would incorporate fundraising into the existing structure, starting with the board. Courtney and her staff could then integrate fundraising expectations into their volunteer recruitment, training, and leadership development standards and materials.

We started with candid talks about fundraising during board meetings. We didn't ask board members to fundraise. We asked them to share their experiences of how and why they got involved with the agency, why they stayed, and why they got more involved. We needed to get off the quid pro quo mentality of "if you donate to my cause, I'll donate to yours." We practiced sharing stories then asked board members to share their story with five people and report on results. Most of them reported positive experiences, which encouraged other board members to also reach out.

It worked because we asked them to share their enthusiasm for the mission and not their need for money. The money was just the vehicle to better serve the mission. We decided to tap into the organization's large volunteer base to get more people asking, basing their messages on the mission rather than the agency's need.

To do this, staff needed to revise their volunteer recruitment, training, and leadership development materials to include messages volunteers could use when talking about the nonprofit or their volunteer work at the organization. The messages needed to be consistent with those the board members were hearing. That way, everyone was on the same page, and the board, staff, and volunteers would communicate consistent messages.

Another suggestion was investing in new fundraising software. The current donor-tracking system could not accommodate a large influx of new donors well. Several excellent, low-cost options on the market would fit their needs.

The first thing we did to excite the community about its mission was to identify the target group leadership wanted to reach, in this case, people who were in their thirties and forties, as opposed to the people in their fifties who comprised most of the board and sixties and older who comprised most of the donor base. We did some research and learned how the different age cohorts were different from one another. We looked at the different generational histories, needs, values, goals, and communication preferences. Then we designed a communications outreach program that the younger cohort would be more likely to respond to.

We worked on messaging together. We created a case for support that reflected the needs, values, and goals of the cohort we were trying to reach. We revised fundraising materials to be consistent with the case for support and its messaging, including their annual campaign, major gift materials, and website content.

We also worked on PR and communications. Luckily, the agency was in the process of hiring a part-time social media specialist who was tech-savvy and identified with the younger age group. Courtney shared the case for support with her and directed her to develop posts consistent with it.

Because this nonprofit had deep relationships with their community, the executive director and board members asked their contacts to help spread the word about the agency. Since the case for support highlighted the benefits to the community, they shared the case for support, which was received well. Area businesses posted flyers in their windows, volunteers put signs on their lawns, and the local press featured them multiple times. Since they had unified messaging, the community got a clear sense of who the organization was, what it stood for, and the benefits of engaging with it.

It wasn't long before the organization started to attract the attention of younger people. And the agency started to collect information about their younger supporters through their interactions with them. Soon, they converted some of that support into dollars and cents.

During our engagement, the nonprofit realized more than an 8 percent increase in individual donations and a 15 percent increase in the number of donors. It also started to acquire the support from younger people it wanted. As of this writing, the positive trends continue.

Board members remain excited about sharing their stories and are more comfortable approaching their connections. They are out of the "you give to mine; I'll give to yours" asking mentality they were in. And they are recruiting and onboarding new board members accordingly.

The staff is working according to the fundraising plan we developed, without being overly taxed. The agency's donor retention rate remains high. The organization has a date scheduled for its new donor software system installation.

The organization's volunteer recruitment and training tools, fundraising materials, outreach instruments, and website have incorporated the new messaging. The agency continues to use the communication channels that best reach younger people while maintaining the channels that their older donors like.

The community is responding positively. More people are fundraising for them, and younger people have started to contribute financially. Exactly what they wanted.

Wrapping It Up

To successfully implement a strong fundraising system, you need a strategy that capitalizes on your nonprofit's strengths and works within the limits of your agency's capacity. The goal is keeping expenses to a minimum while raising revenues, thus increasing return on investment.

Emphasizing mission is the key to asking for money. Your mission is something that rallies your board and excites your community. The Sustainable High ROI Fundraising System helps you create an organizational culture where board and staff become consistent mission ambassadors. Board members and staff leaders work together in a supportive relationship to attract more donors and attain higher donations.

You must also set up your staff for success, providing them with the resources they need to do their jobs. You need a fundraising plan that includes all factors affecting its operations, including technology, communications, campaigns and appeals, staffing, and board involvement.

As you raise awareness of your nonprofit in the community, you will attract more advocates to your cause. These advocates can then be galvanized to spread the word about your agency. As people become excited about your mission, they can be asked to further your cause. As they respond, you will realize increased financial support. Which you can pour back into your mission. Meeting more mission encourages more community support and your sustainability cycle has begun.

Points to Remember

- The Sustainable High ROI Fundraising System involves thoroughly assessing your nonprofit's fundraising strengths and gaps, engaging your board so they willingly fundraise, equipping your staff with the tools necessary to meet your financial and mission goals, and enthusing your community about your cause.

- When you apply The Sustainable High ROI Fundraising System you will uncover immediate ways to raise more money, get staff and board working together in their respective roles, realize increased community support, recruit new donors, see increasingly larger donations, reduce your overall fundraising costs, and enjoy ongoing net surpluses.

What's Next

Now that we've reviewed the four components that comprise the sustainable high ROI fundraising system, we turn our attention to applying it. My goal throughout the rest of the book is to show you how to build the infrastructure you need to achieve sustainability without a heavy lift on existing resources. In other words, how to put a fundraising system in place that works within your organizational capacity and where you realize sustainable financial and mission growth. In the next chapter, we start by exploring the efficient fundraising plan.

Chapter Three

Creating Fundraising Efficiencies

Marc through up his hands in despair. "No matter what I do, I can never seem to get financially ahead. It seems the agency is always treading water, no matter how much fundraising we do."

I understood. His counseling agency was not unique. I had heard this before.

"What have you already done to meet your goals?" I asked.

"My staff and I are working as hard as we can. We all put in extra hours. And our results are good. Last year we raised $1 million through our fundraising efforts. We just can't ever seem to get ahead." How could we turn around Marc's situation?

Defining Efficiency

Investopedia defines efficiency as "the peak level of performance using the least amount of inputs to achieve the highest amount of output. Efficiency requires reducing the number of unnecessary resources to produce a given output. It is a measurable concept that can be determined using the ratio of useful output to total input. It minimizes the waste of resources, such as physical materials, personal energies, and time, while accomplishing the desired output." Merriam-Webster's definition is much simpler. It defines efficiency as "the ability to do or produce something without wasting materials, time, or energy."

Achieving financial, marketing, and work efficiencies is what The Sustainable High ROI Fundraising System is all about. Return on investment is an efficiency measure. Applied to fundraising, it is calculated by dividing fundraising net income by total fundraising costs (see **Appendix A**). It involves the analysis of both revenues and expenses and can also be applied to the time and effort spent on implementing each fundraising activity.

Creating fundraising efficiencies is one way you increase organizational capacity without taxing resources because you are getting rid of waste. Integrating these efficiencies into how you budget, delegate tasks, evaluate performance, form alliances, and pursue funding is all part of implementing step two of the Sustainable High ROI Fundraising System—mobilizing your staff and setting them up to succeed.

Achieve a Net Surplus

It is in overall net surpluses that you find money to put in reserves, invest in your agency's future, and expand organizational capacity, advancing your agency's mission. You should always budget for an overall surplus.

To ensure you realize positive net income, it is good practice to budget your expenses 5 percent higher than you think they will be and budget revenues 5 percent lower than you think they will be while still projecting positive net income. It is how your nonprofit will financially grow.

To create a budget surplus, craft your revenue budgets before you develop your expense budgets. That way, operational capacity is in line with income generation capacity. It does you no good to state unrealistic fundraising income projections. If your income projections are overstated, you will end up failing to meet your budget, realizing negative net income, and getting grief from your board because you are not meeting expectations.

A healthy overall agency surplus is 3 to 6 percent of your operating budget. Individual department, program, event, and other activity budgets may break

Encouragement

Based on past results, you can achieve a 3–6 percent overall agency surplus by implementing The Sustainable High ROI Fundraising System and realizing its resource efficiencies.

even, though. That's fine, as long as you realize overall positive net income. Just make sure, the different budgets maintain internal consistency.

Find Hidden Resources

Increasing revenues is not the only way to increase net income. There are many leadership, management, and financial interventions that uncover hidden resources that lead to improved financial performance. Tapping into those resources does not require spending money, yet you still increase capacity.

Create a Strengths-Based Culture

A strengths-based culture focuses on developing individual and team strengths, rather than emphasizing the correction of weaknesses. It maximizes the efficiency of an organization, increasing the productivity of employees, heightening the ultimate success of the agency. You end up with a better return on the time and effort you've invested in employee development. Agency costs also go down.

People are happier when their strengths are recognized and appreciated. Their attitude toward work is more positive, resulting in a more enjoyable work environment. Their mental health and wellbeing improve. Less sick days are used, increasing productivity and reducing costs.

> **Words of Wisdom**
>
> A happy employee is a motivated employee.

Developing individual and team strengths creates tremendous opportunity for growth. Because interactions are positive, there is less friction between supervisors and workers. It also takes less time and effort to train someone in a task that builds on their strengths because the work comes naturally to them. In addition, it takes less time for workers to complete tasks that come naturally to them. And employees are more engaged in work they enjoy and are given the freedom to do. Productivity increases.

Recognizing their strengths also accepts people for who they are. It acknowledges them for their contributions, making them feel a valued, important part of the organization. Loyalty increases. Retention goes up. Turnover costs go down.

The benefits of employing a strengths-based approach with your fundraising team are even greater. According to a recent study by the Association for Fundraising Professionals, the average tenure of a development professional is fourteen months. One of the top reasons they leave is because of toxic work cultures. Everyone on your fundraising team—development staff, board, and volunteers—are much more likely to stick around if the work environment is cheerful, appreciative, and accepting.

Engage in Strategic Planning

A strategic plan gives arms and legs to your vision of the future. It is a working document, used to guide decisions regarding mission advancement. It can also be used as the basis for structuring organizational culture shifts, uniting board and staff around the language and concepts that enable them to become consistent mission ambassadors.

Research has shown that nonprofits with written strategic plans are more likely to meet their mission and financial goals. A strategic plan defines a nonprofit's overall direction and the resources allocated toward meeting its objectives. The strategic plan outlines an agency's current position, their vision for the future, their values, their priorities, the methods they will employ to achieve their vision, how they define success, and how they evaluate success. A strategic plan looks at the organization from an overall perspective while the program, marketing, fundraising, staffing, financial, and risk management plans stemming from it provide detailed implementation tactics to their respective staff and board teams.

Every nonprofit should have a written, updated strategic plan to guide fundraising discussions, facilitate goal setting, and ensure consistent decision making. Research by the Concord Leadership Group found that 49 percent of nonprofits do not have a strategic plan.

Strategic plans build efficiencies through the process by which they are developed and the direction they provide. They coordinate activities between people and groups. A strategic plan will integrate fundraising with other organizational functions, improving communication, leveraging work efforts, and increasing resource utilization. Strategic planning also benefits your agency through formulation of better strategies and solutions to issues you are addressing, in the case of fundraising, acquiring resources. In addition, strategic planning empowers individual workers and teams to explore cross-departmental solutions to any fundraising matters that may arise, for example, the receiving, recording, and reconciling of donations.

Foster Collaboration

Collaboration, true collaboration, produces synergy where the sum of the whole is greater than its parts. In other words, 1 + 1 = 3. This synergy can be created through agency-to-agency partnerships.

Agency-to-agency collaborations leverage limited resources, achieving higher efficiencies. Let's face it – there are only so many resources available and competition for those resources is fierce. When nonprofits compete rather than collaborate with one another, resources are wasted on duplication of services. Many funders are tired of this situation and therefore require collaboration between organizations. So, rather than be a solo player and try to garner resources to move your individual agency forward, you actually end up with more resources when you apply for funding as a group and share what is given. It's the old story of stone soup, where all inhabitants of the town were poor but by each contributing what they had, they ended up with something much healthier that benefitted everyone.

Notice, though, that all the townspeople had to contribute something they already possessed. Maybe not much, but they had to give up something, nonetheless. It's hard when you're a resource-strapped agency to give something up. That's part of the reason collaborations are so hard. We want to keep the resources we have worked so hard to obtain.

> **Important Point**
>
> More and more of today's funders require collaboration among nonprofits.

Another is trust. In order to collaborate, we must trust that each party involved will fulfill their part of the bargain, and that kind of trust takes time to build. Time executive directors don't have. Or, rather, don't make the time to have.

When I was an executive director, a group of us started a consortium of executive directors to specifically increase the nonprofit capacity within our county. We met monthly. We started with organizing an annual conference for other executive directors. As we did, we got to know each other and developed relationships with one another. Then we started partnering agency-to-agency, which led to resources being brought into our different organization that promoted our respective missions and improved our respective capacities. Which increased our prospects for funding. Which increased our chances for funding. Which, eventually, led to more funding. Those monthly meetings were well worth our time.

Agency-to-agency partnerships can also create economies of scale. Economies of scale are achieved when the unit costs of producing a product or service decrease. For example, it costs less per unit to manage a hundred apartment units than five. So, management companies crop up that serve several smaller apartment complexes through the same apartment manager to achieve an economy of scale.

With nonprofits, economies of scale can be achieved through things like bulk supply buying, sharing large spaces, or any other arrangements that can reduce operating costs on a per unit basis. For example, I've seen larger nonprofits manage the accounting, IT, or human resource functions of smaller nonprofits. The larger nonprofit benefits through the increased revenues from the smaller nonprofit. The smaller nonprofit benefits from lower general operating costs than what they would otherwise generate.

Reduce Costs

The fastest and least expensive way to increase net income is to reduce costs since cost cutting can usually be done immediately and without financial investment. Look at both direct and indirect fundraising costs. Direct costs are those that are directly related to the activity you are implementing. Indirect costs, sometimes known as general and administrative or overhead expenses, are those resources that the activities need to be successful but are part of overall agency expenses.

When you look at your indirect costs, you want to look at your fundraising operational expenses like your banking fees, credit card fees, and donor management and software costs, among others. Then look at your organizational general operating costs—for example, office supplies and janitorial costs. To realize more net income, you may want your fundraising strategy to include negotiating with vendors who provide these products and services. The relationship you start may surprise you.

I once asked the president of a bank who was interested in making a charitable contribution for a reduced rate of interest on our loans as opposed to a grant contribution. Win-win. The bank got its community reinvestment credits and we saved $250,000 over the life of the loan. Not only that, but the next year I went back with a grant request and that was funded too. One year, the bank even gave me more than I requested! Talk about a win.

There are ways to decrease costs that have better long-term results than others. If you have to cut costs, cut them in a way that will bring you the most long-term benefit. For example, making across the board percentage cuts doesn't work as well as more fine-tuned strategic cuts.

> **Food for Thought**
>
> There are ways to decrease costs that have better long-term results than others.

Don't cut anything that yields a good return on investment, such as a donor database. You might not need the most expensive one out there, but you do need a donor database that will do what you need it to do, like integrate your mailing, donor, and volunteer lists. Likewise, a foundation and grants database is a good investment, saving hours of time spent in grant research. Both technologies pay off in spades in terms of saved time.

Sometimes training is seen as an optional expense. Not true. Studies show that fundraisers who receive more training yield better fundraising results. Those few hundred dollars your agency spends on networking events, conferences, and webinars may be helping you realize thousands of dollars in more efficient fundraising operations through the improved fundraising techniques picked up during those networking and training experiences.

Another fundraising cost often considered frivolous is administrative support. Properly executing fundraising activities involves many administrative tasks. There are donations to enter and mailing lists to keep updated. There are reports to run. There are acknowledgement letters to be sent. There are invitations to design and send out. There are RSVPs to track. There may be seating charts or golf foursomes to create. There are supplies to order. There are name tags to make. There are grants to copy, including large attachments like 990s and audits. If you're pursuing government contracts, there's even more paperwork. There are also phone calls to field, questions to answer, and appointments to make. If you are responsible for communications too, you also have newsletters to format and email campaigns to manage. Administrative support is crucial to efficient fundraising operations. Look at it from a cost perspective. Who costs you more: a fundraising professional or an administrative assistant? How much money are you *not* making while your fundraising professional is engaged in administrative work?

Consider Changing Your Revenue Mix

There are many activities to choose from: you can write a grant, bid for an upcoming government contract, implement another fundraising event, help board members cultivate major donors, educate a politician about the needs of your clients and the impact legislative polices have on them, initiate an email campaign, or prepare a direct mailing. The list goes on. There are an infinite number of things you can do to raise money.

Food for Thought

The question is not, "How much can I do?" The question is, "What activities can I do more of that will bring me the most return on my investment?"

Face it. You and your team, be it staff or volunteers, have limited time. Time is your most precious commodity. The question is not, "How much can I do?" The question is, "What activities can I do more of that will bring me the most return on my investment? How can I shape my mix of fundraising activities so that they are the most profitable they can be as a whole?"

The answer is to compare returns on investment. To calculate return on investment, divide net income by expenses for each fundraising activity (see **Appendix A**). What are your results? Where is your highest return on investment? What activities do you do that bring in the most amount of money using the least amount of resources?

Maybe writing that extra grant delivers a higher financial return on investment than implementing that small fundraiser. Maybe you find that soliciting major gifts is your highest return on investment, higher even than writing grants. Maybe you find your Facebook campaign delivers your highest return on investment. Whatever it is, that's where you focus your resources when you have choices to make.

But you want to make sure not to put all your eggs in one basket. You need a diversified revenue portfolio so that if one revenue stream falls through, for whatever reason, you have others to fill in the gap.

It's not only about money though. It is mission that motivates donors to give. Individuals are motivated by mission fulfillment. Foundations are looking for mission matches. Businesses are looking for partners with a strong sense of corporate identity, which, for a nonprofit, is mission fulfillment. It's not all about money. It's about mission too.

Don't chase solely after the money. Chasing after the money can lead to mission drift. If your organization veers from its mission, you will eventually lose community support. Individual donors won't know what you stand for, you will not meet foundation requirements for meeting your mission, and businesses will pick up on your weak organizational identity.

Practically speaking, what does mission-oriented fundraising look like? Mission-oriented fundraising is talking to your donors about community needs, not the needs of your organization. It's applying to foundations with matching missions as opposed to big payouts. It's implementing events that fulfill your mission just as much as they raise money. Always stay true to your mission. Always. Your fundraising will be more successful for it.

Once you look at mission and financial performance, some of your fundraising activities may not be working for you in the way you want them to. Maybe they are very mission-oriented but losing money. Or maybe they're making a lot of money but aren't related to your mission. Well, there's an additional filter you use to judge the return on investment of your fundraising activities: the impact filter. What kind of impact does each activity make?

For example, how much mission do those grants or government contracts fulfill? Probably a lot. Do they make money? Maybe not. Maybe they break even, or even cost more to implement than you receive. If they are core to your mission, it may be worth it to you to subsidize losses with other fundraising activities that are making you money. Or it may not.

How much community awareness does that gala or walk generate? Maybe a lot. You might want to keep them, infuse them with mission, and look at ways you can increase the net income they produce.

What are your other organizational goals? Are you trying to more comprehensively meet client needs? Are you looking to recruit more advocates for your cause? Is one of your goals to provide networking opportunities between government officials and major donors to help solidify important relationships? Do you want your business donors to get to know your clients, so they better understand your mission? Exactly what are your goals in terms the impact you want to make through each fundraising activity? You might have a good reason to give up high profits for high impact.

By the way, there are no right or wrong answers. It all depends on the goals and annual objectives stated in your agency's strategic plan, a hidden resource we addressed above.

Emphasize Donor Retention over Acquisition

According to Fundraising Effectiveness Project data, the average overall donor retention rate hovers right around 46 percent. That means that of every one hundred donors a nonprofit gains, it loses sixty-four. And if it costs more than a dollar to realize every dollar gained, your heavy emphasis on donor recruitment is costing you more than you are realizing in net income. Since it costs more to acquire new donors than retain current ones, a shift in strategy from an emphasis on donor acquisition to an emphasis on donor retention may well be the most cost-beneficial way to improve fundraising performance.

For example, say you have a donor retention rate of 45 percent and raise $75,000. Fifty percent of your total comes from existing donors and 50 percent from new donors. Your average cost to retain a donor is 20 cents and to acquire a donor is $1.20. Your net campaign results will be only $22,500, far less than the $75,000 you grossed.

	Amount Raised	Average cost to Raise $1	Total Cost to Raise	Final Results
45% retained donors	$37,500	$0.20	$7,500	$30,000
65% new donors	$37,500	$1.20	$45,000	($7,500)
Total	$75,000	-	$52,500	*$22,500*

However, say that your donor retention rate is 80 percent, and you only raise $50,000, $25,000 less than your previous total. Your average cost to retain a donor is still 20 cents and to acquire a donor is $1.20. Your campaign net results will now be $30,800.

You just raised what seems like less money but really isn't. Even though you grossed only 67 percent of what you did before, you netted $8,300 more. And you went through a lot less time and effort raising it. Talk about resource efficiency!

	Amount Raised	Average cost to Raise $1	Total Cost to Raise	Final Results
80% retained donors	$40,000	$0.20	$8,000	$32,000
20% new donors	$10,0000	$1.20	$11,200	($1,200)
Total	$50,000	-	$19,200	*$30,800*

So, work on your donor retention efforts just as much, if not more, than your donor acquisition activities.

Reduce Opportunity Costs

Opportunity costs are the costs you incur by *not* doing something else. When it comes to resource development, opportunity costs are related to the time you and your staff spend on various fundraising activities and tasks. For example, special events are very time and labor intensive. It typically costs about fifty cents, not counting labor and overhead, to raise a dollar through fundraising events. Does implementing events prevent you from doing other things that would bring you a higher return on your efforts? Are there other fundraising vehicles that will bring you greater returns on your dollar, be more mission infused, and create a more significant impact? Your goal is to create as much efficiency as you can, given what you're trying to do.

Opportunity cost analysis can also be applied to your staffing structure. For example, to realize the highest return on your staffing dollar, you want to make sure your development director has access to good administrative support. You don't want your primary revenue generator spending too much time on administrative tasks that can be done more efficiently, effectively, and at less cost by an administrative assistant. Of course, it may not be someone totally dedicated to development. But there needs to be someone who can take care of the mailings, do the copying, coordinate meeting and event logistics, enter data, order supplies, and run reports, among other things. In my experience, nonprofits underinvest in administrative support. A good administrative assistant, though, is worth the investment.

Run your own numbers. Remember to account for time and labor costs in your analysis. And then compare the returns on investment. By focusing on those fundraising and staffing elements with the highest financial return, you will expend the least amount of resources to achieve your goals, reducing your overall fundraising costs.

Advocate for Your Plan

Once you understand how to implement the tools necessary for success, you may have to get the changes you want to make through your board. The board approves the annual budget, including fundraising allocations. Your fundraising plan may incorporate some of the changes we have talked about in this chapter, for example changing your revenue mix to achieve better returns on your investment or emphasizing donor retention more than donor acquisition. Board members may be wary of the budget. It may be different than what has been done before. How do you get board members on board?

Ensuring Your Investment Pays Immediate Dividends

As I state in my companion book *The Sustainable High ROI Fundraising System*, the board's job with respect to fundraising is to strategically allocate resources and monitor their acquisition. They should be asking questions like:

- Are we fulfilling our duties to provide resources to implement and grow our mission?

- What strategies are we going to allocate resources toward to meet our mission?

- Do we have a written updated strategic plan that we regularly review and update?

- Are we constantly promoting mission in all we do, even in our fundraising strategy?

- Have we provided a favorable environment for the executive director and staff to succeed in raising money? For example, do we have written board giving and gift acceptance policies in place that we enforce?

- Where will we realize the most financial and mission return on our investment in fundraising?

- How do we want the community to interact with us? How do we as a board influence them to respond the way we want them to?

- Are we making progress in meeting our mission and financial goals?

If they are asking those questions and you have prepared a fundraising plan that increases mission fulfillment and overall net income, abides by your organizational values, raises your nonprofit's visibility, and engages the community in your cause, the board should jump at what you present. Because you will meet the totality of the goals the board has set.

That's why it's important to run the numbers. So, you have actual dollars and cents you can point to behind your assertions. And board members' can base their decisions on objective data rather than gut feelings or emotions.

Calming Board Members' Fears

Of course, there may still be an emotional reaction, especially if you are suggesting a change to the way things have been done before. Change generally elicits an emotional reaction, usually fear. People are most comfortable with the familiar, even if it's not working for them anymore. The familiar is known, the result from a suggested change is not. So, our tendency is to keep doing the same things, with slight variations, expecting different results. It doesn't work that way, though. If you want different results, you must do things differently. And that means change.

If you are suggesting a change, you not only need objective evidence supporting it, but you must also address the emotions behind it. We talk about strategies for dealing with change in **Chapter Fifteen**.

Investing Board Members in the Outcome

You address their emotions before you address the objectivity of your data. Calm their fears first, so they can hear you. Strong emotions can cloud rational thought. When that happens, logic goes out the window. So, address the emotions first, then get down to the facts.

And let them discover the facts. Even if you know the answers, let them discover the facts. Let them come to their own conclusions. For example, you can present your calculations and let them discuss their merits and benefits to the agency and see how what you're proposing increases your organization's mission impact. Remind them of their passion for sitting on the board – mission fulfillment. Let them see how they are changing the world through their decisions. Invest them in their own outcomes.

Marc's Solution

Marc wanted to see results. He wanted to move his fundraising beyond where it was now. He wanted to see the financial fruits of all his labor.

The first thing I did was a revenue and cost analysis. What I found was that, although Marc's team raised $1 million dollars, it took them $1.1 million to do it. Mark needed to cut fundraising costs, change his revenue mix to be more efficient, or a combination of both. The counseling center was already operating lean and mean. There wasn't much more meat to be cut off the bone without sacrificing quality, something Marc was unwilling to do. The answer, then, was to increase fundraising efficiency. And do it without adding costs.

As a former counselor, Marc understood the importance of using a strengths-based approach to solve problems, He had already successfully integrated that perspective into all aspects of his organizational culture. Marc also had an up-to-date strategic plan that guided his staff's work and that he reviewed regularly. But as an agency, the center was pretty insular in terms of community collaborations. It had also never looked at efficiency metrics.

I suggested Marc make a list of what he had to offer other nonprofits and the organizational needs he needed met. Then I suggested he reach out to other executive directors and develop relationships. Perhaps the respective nonprofits had synergy where both could offer something of value and benefit by collaborating with one another.

I also suggested the Marc change his fundraising emphasis from donor recruitment to donor retention. The agency's donor retention rate hovered around 50 percent, better than average but not by much.

Finally, I recommended Marc move his fundraising strategy from one of many special events to less events and more large personal gifts.

Marc decided to pursue the community collaborations. He was also eager to run the numbers so that he could present data-based evidence for making budget allocation changes to the board.

Within the year, the counseling center realized a fundraising net surplus.

Wrapping It Up

It is net surpluses that fund your nonprofit's reserves, investment in your agency's future, and increases in organizational capacity. Strive for an annual 3-6 percent operating margin. To get there, tap into your agency's hidden resources. Create a healthy, strengths-based work culture. Fundraising staff, board, and volunteers are much more likely to stick around if the work environment is cheerful, appreciative, and accepting. Engage in strategic planning. Strategic plans coordinate activities between people and groups, integrating fundraising with other organizational functions, improving communication and leveraging work efforts. Collaborate with other nonprofits in the community. Agency-to-agency partnerships leverage limited resources.

Pay attention to the bottom line. If you have to cut costs, cut them in a way that will bring you the most long-term benefit. Don't cut anything that yields a good return on investment. Compare the returns on investment of your fundraising options. Plan activities that bring in the most amount of money using the least amount of resources, promote your mission, and make the impact you desire. To improve your overall financial results, focus on improving your donor retention rate. On average, of every hundred donors a nonprofit gains, it loses sixty-four, costing them in net income. Don't let this happen to you. And pay attention to your opportunity costs. Remember to account for time and labor in your cost analyses.

The board's job with respect to fundraising is to strategically allocate resources and monitor their acquisition. If they are asking strategic questions and you meet the totality of their goals, your fundraising plan should be well received. Their goals include greater mission fulfillment, higher net income, improved visibility, and increased community support, all achieved with authenticity.

If you want different results, you must do things differently. And that means suggesting a change, which generally elicits an emotional reaction, usually fear. If you are suggesting a change, you not only need objective evidence supporting it, but you must also address the emotions behind it. Calm their fears so they can hear you. And let them discover the facts and come to their own conclusions. You want them invested in their own outcomes.

Points to Remember

- To ensure a fundraising net surplus, budget your fundraising expenses 5 percent higher than you think they will be and revenues 5 percent lower than you think they will be.

- You find hidden resources at no additional cost by creating a strengths-based culture, engaging in strategic planning, fostering collaborations, eliminating unnecessary costs, changing your revenue mix, emphasizing donor retention just as much as donor acquisition, and reducing your opportunity costs.

- To get board members onboard with instituting fundraising changes, run the numbers so they have objective data on which to make decisions, calm their fears, and let them discover the facts.

What's Next

Now that you are equipped with the tools you need to generate fundraising efficiencies, we turn our attention to moving the system forward. In the next chapter, we explain the role mindset plays in determining fundraising success and how it can leverage resources.

Chapter Four

Kill the Scarcity Mindset

S tacey sighed as she hung up the phone. It was another donor wondering how his donation was being used. The previous executive director had asked for donations based on the drug prevention agency's need for money for quite a few years. As a result, the community saw the nonprofit as poor and struggling. Many donors had stopped giving because they didn't know if the organization would survive.

Board members' morale was low. The agency's financial reserves were gone. In fact, Stacey was projecting a substantial loss by the end of the year. The drug prevention agency never got the big donations. The real money went to the large treatment facilities and there just wasn't enough to go around. The future did not look good. How was Stacey going to turn things around?

Assessing Mindset

When you assess your nonprofit's fundraising strengths and gaps, you will find things that both encourage and inhibit board members' involvement in spreading mission and fundraising, your staffs' ability to succeed, and how your organization interacts with the community. To create an action plan that shows you how to take the next step toward financial stability and mission impact, you have to have the right attitude. This chapter looks at the power your mindset has in successfully moving The Sustainable High ROI System forward. We define the scarcity and abundance mentalities, the effects of mindset on meeting your fundraising goals, and how to overcome a debilitating outlook.

Steven Covey coined the words 'scarcity mentality' and 'abundance mindset' in his book ***The 7 Habits of Highly Successful People***. The theory is that your mindset determines your success. Which is a theory backed up by quantitative research. In her research with young students, Stanford psychologist Carol Dweck found that children with the mindset that intelligence is unlimited and can be developed, overcame academic challenges better than children with the mindset that intelligence is predetermined and finite. And a study of middle-aged adults by researchers at Yale and Miami Universities found that those with more positive beliefs around aging lived seven and a half years longer than those with less positive perceptions.

You can apply the principles of the scarcity and abundance mindsets to your own success in leading your nonprofit forward and garnering the resources you need to advance your agency's mission.

The Scarcity Mindset

The scarcity mindset is a belief that there is a finite number of resources in the universe for which people and organizations compete. Life is a competition for fixed resources and there are winners and losers in the game. When one person or organization gets a large piece of the pie, by necessity, everyone else gets a smaller piece of the pie. This mindset becomes a problem when you focus on your lack of resources to the exclusion of anything else.

Which is easy to do. Most of us have been conditioned to think in these terms: colleges and universities admit a fixed number of new students, promotions and raises are scarce, budgets are limited, and there is only so much time. Scarcity thinking is the norm.

Especially when it comes to nonprofits and fundraising. There are, in fact, only so many foundations who give fixed amounts each year. And the government, constrained by its budget, enters into only a limited number of contracts each year. There are only 24 hours in day. It is understandable why nonprofits constantly describe themselves as underfunded, without the necessary resources to adequately meet their missions. To some extent, scarcity is real. And competition for funding is fierce.

But if you focus on what you don't have and your fundraising rallying cry is, "Help us, please. We need your donation to survive," then you're in trouble.

Because if you are focusing on what you don't have, you never even think of other solutions. The tunnel vision of the scarcity mindset affects your ability to solve problems, think logically, and make decisions. It limits your ability to plan, trapping you in short-term thinking. To make matters worse, because your brain is too busy thinking about what you don't have, you are more prone to give into your impulses, using up precious resources and continuing your situation of being without. It's a self-fulfilling prophecy and confirmation of the belief that you won't ever have all you need. In worst-case circumstances, I have seen nonprofits give up and stop trying, resigning themselves to their current situation.

You hear the scarcity mindset at work in statements like:

- "They always get the money."

- "We never get the money."

- 'We don't have enough money."

- "We can't achieve that."

But there is hope. There is another way to look at things that leads to more successful outcomes.

The Abundance Mindset

The abundance mindset is the opposite of the scarcity mindset. The abundance mindset is the belief that there is enough for everyone. Instead of seeing one pie being divvied up, you see the possibility of making another pie. Rather than competition producing winners and losers, you see it producing more and more value, for example, more knowledge, skill, and experience. Life is not a win-lose proposition with the abundance mentality. You believe you can always find a win-win solution.

> ## Food for Thought
>
> Although resources are perceived to be scarce, there are actually enough for everyone. Think in terms of collaborating with others to share resources instead of always directly receiving them. Let the law of synergy kick in.

The abundance mindset is characterized by thinking big. In other words, having vision. You are driven by the belief that you aren't stuck with what you have and can improve with effort. You know your strengths and weaknesses. You have an open mind. Your outlook is optimistic. Since you know there's enough to go around, you can afford to be generous with others. You embrace change, acting proactively.

You believe that the world is full of possibility, and you take advantage of opportunities as they present themselves. You plan ahead, thinking in terms of long-term results rather than just short-term outcomes. In other words, you lead your organization forward to a brighter future—and you get there. Like the scarcity mindset, the abundance mindset becomes a self-fulfilling prophecy. Because you see the limitless potential in yourself and everyone around you, you intentionally drive yourself toward reaching the results you want.

If you have an abundance mindset you don't fear resources being taken from you through competition. You tend to engage in collaborative, instead of competitive, relationships. Instead of winners and losers, you want everyone to succeed. You understand that a rising tide lifts all boats and see your collaborators' success as essential to your own. Since you don't fear others taking from you and are invested in others' success, you tend to have supportive relationships and strong social support systems both personally and professionally.

Not that you are an idealist when you look at things. You are grounded in reality. You are just not limited by what is. In other words, instead of settling for one pie, you make another pie. It is the abundance mindset that drives you forward in creating a new reality.

This means you can see new possibilities, set goals toward those possibilities, and plan an approach that results in meeting your goals.

Comparing the Scarcity and Abundance Mindsets

Characteristics of the Scarcity Mindset	Characteristics of the Abundance Mindset
Competitive in nature	Collaborative in nature
Works toward individual gain	Works toward group gain
Tunnel vision	Open mindedness
Short-term thinking	Long-term planning
Create win-lose solutions	Create win-win solutions
Keep resources for oneself	Share resources with others
Envy	Satisfaction
Lethargy	Action orientation

Note that you can lie anywhere on the continuum between the two poles, sharing some scarcity and some abundance mindset characteristics. As pointed out earlier, you have a problem when you focus exclusively on what you don't have rather than what you do have.

How the Two Mindsets Show Up in Fundraising

When it comes to fundraising, how do the two mindsets manifest themselves?

The scarcity mentality says there are winners and losers in the funding game. For example, bigger nonprofits always get a disproportionate amount of the available funding and squeeze the smaller nonprofits to the point where they find it hard to survive.

The abundance mentality says you can learn and be inspired by those who get the funding. Perhaps you can approach the bigger nonprofits and collaborate in some form where you share resources. Say, by becoming a subcontractor in a community project. Or maybe jointly creating an advocacy campaign that you share with your respective constituencies so that both your nonprofits' impacts are multiplied.

The scarcity mentality is jealous of how much money ABC Nonprofit raised compared to the smaller amount your nonprofit ended up with. You'll never get ahead this way.

The abundance mentality rejoices that you both raised money. You are inspired by ABC Nonprofit's success to exceed your goals next time. You approach ABC Nonprofit asking how you can both take what you got and leverage your resources so that you both get more next time.

With a scarcity mentality, you are secretly happy when a competing nonprofit does not meet their financial goals. Because you assume that means more resources are available to your nonprofit, with a better chance for you to acquire your own needed resources.

The abundance mindset says when ABC Nonprofit is having a hard time acquiring needed resources, putting their contribution to the field at risk, you do what you can to help them reach their goals so you can continue to benefit from their success. You ask how can you partner with them so that both of you reach your financial and mission goals.

Not that this is easy, of course. When it comes to money, people are pretty proprietary. The fear is that your agency will be taken advantage of and lose what it has worked so hard for, putting your survival at risk. A perfect example of how we have been indoctrinated as a society in the scarcity mindset.

Transitioning from the Scarcity to Abundance Mentality

As a leader, your values and belief system will influence and change the organizational culture. (We explore the effects of leadership in **Chapter Thirteen**.) What can you do to not only shift your mentality from scarcity to abundance, but also your board members and staff? And how can you change the negative community perceptions of your nonprofit created as a result of the scarcity mindset?

You

We all get stuck in the scarcity mindset at some point in our lives. To get yourself out of the scarcity mindset and into an abundant mindset:

- Focus on what you do have and let that move you forward.

- Surround yourself with positive people. I know it's hard as an executive director to find colleagues to spend time with. It's lonely at the top. Yet these relationships are your lifeline. Find other executive directors who are positively looking forward to and make time to build relationships with others.

- Practice gratitude. Gratitude has been shown to improve mental health and general well-being.

- Organize your time and systemize tasks that help you meet your long-term goals. For example, schedule time to review your nonprofit's finances at the same time every day, even if it is only fifteen minutes. In the same vein, schedule a regular time to speak with important donors. Don't forget you need to schedule time to nurture relationships with staff and board members, too, even if it is only by walking around and engaging in small talk.

- Get enough sleep, exercise, and eat right. You will feel better for it and your outlook will improve.

- Engage in self-care. Take time away from your desk on a daily basis. Take time off as you need it. When you're off, don't work. Do something non-work related that will rejuvenate and refresh you.

- Ensure time with family and friends. Being an executive director is a hard job. Sometimes you are not your staffs' or board's favorite person. Spend time with people who unconditionally love and accept you.

Your Board

Board members may also exhibit a scarcity mentality. As we said earlier, most of us are conditioned to think in terms of competition. To get board members out of their scarcity mentalities and into an abundant mindset you can:

- Present the glass as half full. For example, you can start board meetings with a client success story or ask each board member what they are grateful for in carrying out their governance duties. Although you can't change the nature of your board members at their core, you can create an environment where your nonprofit's assets are a subject for discussion.

- Maintain a positive attitude during board meetings and in your interactions with board members. Let those board members with a positive attitude contribute to the discussion and not be drowned out by others' negativity. This requires building a collaborative relationship with your board chair, who should be the one facilitating board meetings.

- Make addressing long-term goals a part of every board meeting agenda. So often, board members want to focus on the immediate and the operational. But immediate and operational responsibilities are not your board members' job. They're yours. So, when you do speak to present affairs, use them as launching point for meeting future organizational objectives.

- Build individual relationships with each board member. Be vulnerable with them, letting them know your values and perspective.

- Help board members appreciate the present good no matter what your nonprofit's current circumstances. It's going to be harder for some to see the positives than others. And it's going to take longer for others to accept your positivity than others. Give them the time they need outside of board meetings to think about the issues raised during meetings.

While you can't change board members' natures, you can influence board members' perspectives by building strong relationships that contribute to a positive environment focused on meeting long-term organizational goals.

Your Staff

Like board members, your staff may have also been conditioned to think in terms of scarcity. They are, after all, the ones with so much to do with so little help. To move your staff out of a scarcity mindset and into an abundance mentality:

- Don't demand more and more from your staff. Hire well and recognize what they do give to you. Appreciate a job well done. With authentic gratitude, you will motivate your staff to work even harder. An added bonus is that you will engender their loyalty.

- Take a strengths-based approach when speaking to your staff about getting work done. Start with where they are and move forward from there.

- Reward attitude as much as work product. Find ways to make it clear that you value positivity.

- When giving performance reviews, focus more on what was done than what was not. Let your staff know you recognize and treasure their hard work. Support them as you teach them how to move forward.

- Paint the big picture for them. Caught up in the day-to-day operations, they need someone to point out the larger impact of their work.

- Encourage them to take their lunches, breaks, and time off. You want them to have time to rejuvenate so they have the energy they need to perform their work. Plus, their outlook will improve.

- Model the behavior you want them to imitate. Actions speak louder than words.

As the executive director, you have control over the work environment. You can create a workplace that rewards and encourages positivity and excellence. We talk more about shaping organizational culture in **Chapter Fifteen**.

Your Community

If you, your board members, and your staff have described your nonprofit in terms of the scarcity mindset, your community may see your agency as struggling to make ends meet with no relief in sight. Which is a bad image to have when you are trying to raise money. Very few people want to fund a sinking ship. To shift the community perception of your nonprofit from one of being poor and fragile to one of being strong and capable you can:

- Focus the public on what is positive. Create a vision statement and refer to it when you interact with members of the community. Talk about your organizational assets and plans for moving forward. Speak to how you will use your assets to solve important community problems. Infuse your vision into your public image.

- Create a strong, positive brand. A brand encompasses more than your logo. It also includes thinking about the emotions that are elicited when people see the colors and fonts you've used, the words you choose, the arguments for support you make. You also need to think about how you want people to experience your brand. That is, how easy it is to contact you, how people are greeted, how satisfying interacting with your staff is, and how long it takes to resolve complaints, among other things.

- Teach your staff and board members to repeat your positive messages. As insiders, your staff and board are the best community ambassadors you've got. Expose them to messages you want repeated to the public. Audit your internal recruitment, onboarding, training, and operational materials for consistency in messaging and revise them as needed.

- Position your nonprofit as a leader in the field. Differentiate your agency. Let your community know what your nonprofit does that is different than any other organization like you. Get them excited about helping you fund your agency's cause.

- Emphasize mission over money. It is mission that motivates your donors to give. *Always* put mission first. Always.

It takes a lot of work to move the needle from a negative to positive image. But the results are worth it. For a more detailed discussion about how to garner strong community support, see the ***Nonprofit Quick Guide: The Surprisingly Easy Steps to Receiving Robust Community Support***.

Stacey's Solution

To move forward and raise money effectively, Stacey realized she needed to get her board members out of their scarcity mindset, Stacey needed to take an inventory of all that the nonprofit had, communicate those assets to the board, make a plan to get over the immediate hurdle, and work with the board to develop long-term sustainability.

So, Stacey asked board members to tell her what drew them to the agency, why they stayed, and why they got more involved. Then she asked them what they thought drew their volunteers to them and why the volunteers stayed, even during the bad times. Stacey wanted board members to define the strengths the agency would build on.

It was clear from their discussions that everyone involved with it felt the organization was doing important work, the staff and volunteers were good at what they did, the volunteer experience was extremely satisfying, and that going out of business was not an option. Good. They had things to build on.

Stacey and the board worked on a plan that communicated the agency's ability to meet their mission despite their poor financial situation, the excellence of the services they provided, the fulfillment people felt in carrying out the mission, and the unfailing dedication to being there for their clients. These were resources not every nonprofit had. In some respects, the nonprofit Stacey led had a lot.

The board could finally see past what they didn't have. This breakthrough allowed Stacey and the board members to dream and dream big. Their history of overcoming previous difficulties told them they would succeed. They would survive this financial predicament and, after it was over, they would thrive. They dared to think they could start building toward financial sustainability.

That was the beginning of the turnaround.

Wrapping It Up

The scarcity mentality postulates there are a limited number of resources where some get more, and some get less. Most people in our society have been indoctrinated in the scarcity mindset, see competition as necessary to obtain what they want, and go to lengths to protect what they have acquired. In contrast, the abundance mentality assumes that there are enough resources for everyone to have their share. People with an abundance mindset value collaboration and work toward the success of all. Most people fall somewhere between the two poles. The scarcity mentality becomes a problem when the focus in exclusively on the dire lack of resources. The abundance mindset moves you forward and pushes you to meet your goals.

To transition from a scarcity to abundance mentality, you can focus on what you do have, surround yourself with positive people, practice gratitude, systemize tasks that help you meet long-term goals, and take care of yourself. To help your board move to a more abundant mindset strive to create an environment where your organizational assets are part of the discussion, maintain a positive attitude every time you interact with board members, address long-term objectives during board meetings, and build strong relationships with individual board members.

As an executive director, you have more control over the workplace than the boardroom. To move your staff towards a more abundant mindset, express appreciation for a job well done, take a strengths-based approach when correcting deficiencies, reward positive attitudes, give balanced performance reviews, let them know the big picture impact of their work, encourage them to take care of themselves, and model the behavior you want them to imitate.

If you've positioned your nonprofit as poor and weak, you will not raise as much money as you could otherwise. To change the community's perception of your agency, focus on your organizational assets when you communicate with the public, create a strong brand and brand experience, make messaging consistent throughout all operational documents, differentiate your nonprofit, and emphasize mission when talking about money.

With a more positive outlook, inherent drive to achieve results, and tools to help board and staff shift community perceptions of your nonprofit, you will raise more money for your organization and be able to advance your nonprofit's mission as you desire.

Points to Remember

- Focusing on your nonprofit's assets, forming relationships with optimistic people, being appreciative, routinizing small tasks that help you reach long-term objectives, and engaging in self-care help you shift from a scarcity to abundance mentality and propel your agency forward.

- To move board members' scarcity mindsets to more abundant ones, talk about organizational assets during board meetings, maintain a can-do-it attitude with board members, help board members plan for the future, and develop strong, personal relationships with board members.

- Communicating gratefulness, employing a strengths-based approach, rewarding positivity, providing encouraging feedback during performance reviews, describing staff's organizational and community contribution, and urging and modeling self-care inspires staff to convey organizational advantages to the community.

- It takes a lot of work to change community perceptions about your nonprofit including describing your agency in terms of what it does have, developing a robust image, auditing your internal documents for consistency and revising as necessary, discerning and conveying your agency's uniqueness, and putting mission first when fundraising.

What's Next

Now that we've covered the importance of mindset in leading and moving your organization forward, we turn our attention to creating an organizational environment conducive to success and in which The Sustainable High ROI System best functions.

Chapter Five

Six Crucial Keys to Achieving Success

To meet the growing demand to provide musical experiences to her community, Aimee and her board were in the middle of creating a strategic plan that provided direction on how the small community orchestra would expand. Everyone realized that they needed increased funding to meet their goals.

Aimee and her team pondered several questions. What was the best way for prepare for organizational growth? Would the orchestra expand their staff? If so, how was the agency going to fund additional staff costs? Was there anything else they needed to do to get the biggest bang for their buck? Exactly how would their nonprofit move smoothly into the phase of its development? Aimee needed a firm strategic and operational foundation on which she could successfully lead the organization forward. Aimee took a step back. What was her first step?

Preparing Your Nonprofit for Success

Shared and servant leadership, teamwork, goal setting, planning, evaluation, and risk mitigation are essential keys to successfully implementing The Sustainable High ROI Fundraising System. These six practices lay the foundation for empowering your board, mobilizing your staff, and exciting your community. They shape the environment and set expectations for working together that make board and staff mission enthusiasts and raise the most money possible.

Shared and Servant Leadership

The first key to success we are going to address are the ideas of shared and servant leadership. The philosophy of servant leadership is built on the belief that the most effective leadership is leadership that strives to serve the people you work with rather than exert power and control over them. Shared leadership disperses authority, decision-making, and responsibility among members of a group, giving each individual an opportunity to showcase their expertise. When a servant leadership philosophy is combined with a shared leadership style, you create powerful work teams that work toward a higher, common good. You inspire people to do noble work by contributing the best they have to offer.

Adopting the shared and servant leadership philosophies has many benefits. Because power is shared, team members feel a greater sense of partnership, increasing loyalty. Because people are invested in the outcomes, feel a sense of purpose, and know they are contributing, they become more engaged, paving the way for future success. They are motivated and energized to move forward. In addition, shared decision-making leads to better outcomes. Shared power builds trust and fosters respect. And shared responsibility minimizes workload as team members support you to achieve your common goals.

The benefits that stem from a shared and servant leadership mentality lead to efficiencies that influence fundraising success. For example, your board and staff work as partners to excite your community about supporting your nonprofit. And they do it with passion and energy. You can then see an increase in donations coupled with reduced costs, improved work and financial efficiencies, and a higher return on your fundraising investment. We discussed how to create fundraising efficiencies in **Chapter Three**.

To develop a shared and servant leadership culture:

- Put the needs of your organization, board members, and staff before your own interests. That's not to say you don't engage in self-care. You do. You must still separate your personal and professional lives and not let your professional life interfere with your personal priorities.

- Help team members learn and grow. Develop their skills and optimize their performance. For example, let qualified members of the team lead groups. Lean on their expertise. Foster their leadership. Then don't second guess them. Trust their decisions.

- Maintain an open mind and be willing to learn from others. Encourage diversity of thought. Permit team members to freely express themselves.

- Give team members discretion over their tasks and the resources available to meet them. Press them to use the tools they have at their disposal to meet their goals. Support responsible risk-taking and reward initiative.

- Allow autonomy but clearly define their scope of authority. Clearly define what decisions individuals can and cannot influence.

- See yourself as a staff and board resource rather than a traditional manager.

With the Board

When you are dealing with the board, role confusion is common. Often the board, and sometimes the executive director, doesn't understand the difference between governance and management. If the board takes on management responsibilities, there is no one left to do the important work of governing and the nonprofit flounders. The board may also not know how to view the executive director's role. After all, you are their subordinate as they hired you; you are their equal as an ex-officio board member; and you are their organizational authority, knowing more about agency operations than they do. A shared and servant leadership mindset may help you navigate these uncertain waters.

For example, you and other board members can define your role as a resource to the board. You are there to inform and guide, letting them take the leadership and governance roles they signed up for. (Your development director will also serve as a resource to the board, mainly in their role as staff support to the development committee. We explain the structure and function of the development committee in **Chapter Eleven**.) Assuming a shared and servant leadership stance like this helps board members develop their leadership skills, paves the way for diversity of thought, and encourages open discussion, which, in turn, leads to greater engagement. And who doesn't want an engaged board, especially when it comes to fundraising?

When your board is engaged in fundraising, you raise more money. Board and staff work together to reach out to the community and excite it to give, infusing it with a culture of philanthropy. As we mentioned in **Chapter One**, implementing The Sustainable High ROI Fundraising System is more about creating a philanthropic culture than facilitating transactions about money.

> **Food for Thought**
>
> To help the board focus on their work of governing, define your role as a resource to inform and guide them, letting them take on the leadership and governance roles they signed up for.

Of course, there is more to board relations than role definition. For a detailed discussion about managing relationships with your board see *Love Your Board!: The Executive Directors' Guide to Discovering the Sources of Nonprofit Board Troubles and What to Do About Them* by Mary Hiland, Ph.D.

With the Staff

The shared and servant leadership way of thinking also works well when working with your staff. As you help team members learn and grow, you are developing a highly skilled workforce that is invested in your nonprofit's future. And you create loyalty to the organization, increasing employee retention and reducing turnover costs. As a result, productivity goes up. As staff take responsibility for their own work, they begin to take initiative, adding energy to the team and relieving some of your workload.

And these things are exactly what development professionals are looking for in a work environment. We examine fundraising staff desires and address how to attract high-quality development professionals to your nonprofit in **Chapter Twelve**.

Teamwork

The second key to success we'll delve into is teamwork. You know you are successfully leading the organization when your board and staff function as cohesive teams working together to reach a common goal. You look at the board as a group, the staff as a group, and the organization as a group. All three need to function well.

Characteristics of High Functioning Teams

High functioning teams, including your fundraising team of board members, staff, and volunteers, create work efficiencies, improving your return on investment.

Effective teams:

- Trust each other

- Engage in open and honest communication

- Understand their role

- Feel ownership for their jobs

- Function interdependently

- Foster individual talent

- Make decisions together

- Support responsible risk-taking and change

- Compel mutual accountability

- Resolve conflicts quickly and constructively

We talk at length about structuring, recruiting, and retaining your dream fundraising team of board members, volunteers, and staff in **Chapters Eleven, Twelve, and Thirteen**.

Building Effective Teams

The first step to building a strong team is to define the purpose of the team. What do you want the team to accomplish? Remember, when it comes to fundraising, you want to increase *both* money and mission. You have a dual purpose.

The next step is to assemble the right people to be part of the team. You want team members with diverse experiences and complementary skills and abilities. The different perspectives help team members identify the obstacles to implementation at various points in the process and within the organization.

Then unite them with a clear, inspiring vision. Communicate your vision to the team. Define organizational values and set expectations for working together. This is where the benefits of a shared leadership style will kick in.

Let the team break your vision down into the goals and tasks they see are needed to accomplish the group's overall purpose. Each team member should contribute. This assumes each team member knows why they were chosen to be on the team and what their job entails. If you've assembled the right people, discussions will be lively.

Next, have the team set the milestones they will meet. Let them determine their own workload. Make it clear that each team member is responsible for meeting the objectives of the team. And then hold them accountable for their performance.

Clarifying Point

Give your teams goals to meet but let them define their own objectives and develop their own methods for reaching those goals.

Give the team the tools and support needed to meet their goals. Set them up for success. Offer continuous learning options. Encourage each member to share their knowledge and pass their skills on to others. Mentorship programs, seminars, lectures, and conferences should all be part of your plan to grow your staff.

Monitor the advancement of the team. Regularly review their progress, both independently and as a group. Give them direction as they need it. But let them lead the process. By sharing the leadership role, you will realize more time to attend to other important tasks.

When milestones are reached and the goals of the team have been achieved, celebrate the successes and reward team members for their hard work. Let them know you appreciate their contributions, so they stay motivated and energized to move even further forward, paving the way for even greater success.

Goal Setting

Goal setting is the third key to success we'll cover. To get engagement, when you are working with a group, the goals you set together must be agreed to by all parties. And they must be agreed to in terms of both the process used to establish and meet the goals and the outcomes achieved by reaching the goals. The goals you set should be valued and challenging. The more valued and challenging the goal, the more intensely team members will work to attain it and the more success they will feel once it is realized. These feelings of accomplishment lead to confidence and belief in the group's abilities to move forward.

Formulating Goals

When your team sets goals, give the guidance on how to set SMART goals. SMART goals are specific, measurable, action-oriented, realistic, and time-bound. Have all team members agree on each defining characteristic of each goal. Have them determine how goal attainment will be measured, too. And then have the team leader hold the team accountable for doing what they agreed to.

Clarifying Point

Make your goals

Specific

Measurable

Action-oriented

Realistic

Time-bound

Your ultimate goal when it comes to fundraising is not to raise money. It is to further the mission. The money is just a way to fund your mission. Which is important to remember because the exchange of money is not what motivates your donors. Meeting your mission is.

Which means that your fundraising goal needs to be expressed to your donors in terms of mission attainment and impact.

When you ask a donor to grow your mission via a monetary donation, you still need the goals you set to be SMART. "Helping us meet our mission" is not a good mission goal. How do you define mission success? How much mission do you want to meet? Exactly what are you going to do over what period of time? How will you measure your success? Then you match your donors' abilities to give to how much mission they want to meet. We describe how to ask donors for donations in **Chapter Nine**.

Your fundraising team, though, is going to need financial goals in addition to mission goals. You do need to talk to your team about the dollars and cents and define them SMARTly.

Just like meeting as much mission as possible in not a SMART goal, raising as much money as possible is not either. In the fundraising plan, you need to define exactly how much you want to raise by how many people. Set monetary and participation goals for each fundraising activity you implement.

To set realistic goals, ask, "What have we achieved in the past?" Base goals on objective data, not a budget deficit or a wish list. Look at a year's worth of monthly trends. Analyze the trends and associate each rise or dip with actions your agency took during that time period. Look at what worked and what didn't work. Have your team do more of what worked and not do what didn't work, no matter how beloved any particular activity is. Also account for overall economic trends. What is the environment you operate in? What is realistic given the current state of affairs?

Evaluate your monthly and annual mission and fundraising performance using the metrics you stated in your goals and stated in your development plan. Once the team has met their existing goals, celebrate their success. And then have them set new, higher goals, being SMART about them.

Win-Win Solutions

When a team is formulating their goals, it is important that they be win-win, that is, there is a benefit to everyone. Creating win-win solutions lead to the discovery of options that have not been thought of before and positive working relationships.

Devising goals that result in win-win solutions requires all team members to be flexible and patient during the formulation process. Win-win strategies require time for all team members to express their interests, perspectives, and goals. Of course, to do this, team members need to be aware of their own interests, perspectives, and goals and be willing to share them. Which is where the shared and servant leadership styles become so important. You need your team to trust one another and communicate freely, openly, and honestly.

To create win-win goals:

1. Recognize and acknowledge team member differences.

2. Focus on what everyone has in common.

3. See things from others' points of view.

4. Work to overcome conflicts.

5. Develop a plan of action.

6. Follow up.

Planning

Planning, the fourth key to success we'll talk about, is the process we undertake to outline the activities and resources needed to meet our goals. Planning increases the efficiency of your organization, coordinating and organizing resources. It also reduces the risks involved in moving forward. The overarching plan is the strategic plan from which all other management plans are derived.

The Sustainable High ROI Fundraising System assumes the overall purpose of a nonprofit is to increase mission impact through its financial, program, staff, and donor growth. In other words, money is not raised for the sake of finances but with the underlying intent to meet more mission. Yes, implementing the system will improve your nonprofit's financial position. But that is just a means to an end. The end goal is to expand mission impact.

Planning for Financial Growth

If you want to increase your mission impact, you need to grow your finances. It is money that funds mission implementation.

Assessing Financial Needs

A thorough financial assessment is more than a financial audit performed by a CPA or a budget performance review done by the board. It is a review of the strategic plan as it pertains to your financial plan with an accompanying analysis of available fundraising options. For that to happen, you need finance and development to work together.

Finance and Development Interrelationships

You want to make sure that all the goals outlined in the strategic plan are carried through to the financial plan. And by financial plan, I mean a blueprint of how your nonprofit will not only manage its finances but also how it will generate its revenues. Which means that development and finance need to coordinate their financial and development plans.

Furthermore, the fundraising plan should be coordinated with your total organizational budget, not just the development department. You want your fundraisers to be aware of total organizational needs so they can best broker your needs as an agency with the kinds of impact donors want to make. And a fundraiser only knows that by having a complete understanding of the total needs of the organization.

The relationship looks like this:

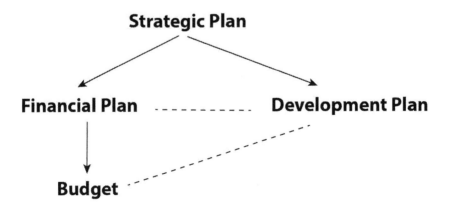

Financial and Fundraising Decision Metrics

We covered the basic financial metrics to calculate in **Chapter Three**, including net income, return on investment, and donor retention rate. Other metrics that will influence decision making are cost to raise a dollar, donor acquisition rate, average gift per donor, and average cost per donor, discussed more thoroughly in the ***Nonprofit Quick Guide: Raising Lots of Money: Essential Measures to Grow Your Finances and Excel at Fundraising***.

Trends in net income indicate your nonprofit's ability to realize a surplus. Cost to raise a dollar tells you how many resources your nonprofit expends to realize one dollar in revenue. Return on investment expresses how well your resources are financially performing. Your donor retention rate reveals the percentage of your total agency donors that made a second or subsequent gift. Your donor acquisition rate articulates the rate of growth of your donor base. Trends in your average gift per donor communicate the level of engagement your donors have with your organization. Trends in average cost per donor divulges how well you are applying fundraising efficiencies when asking for gifts. Studying these metrics helps you weigh the pros and cons of each fundraising endeavor and figure out the best mix and volume of activities to implement to most efficiently and effectively realize your fundraising and mission goals.

Another important metric to consider is donor lifetime value. Donor lifetime value is a measure of how much your donors will contribute on average to your nonprofit over their lifetime span of giving, that is, from first donation to final donation. It is not an exact number. It is an estimate that gives you a good idea of what fundraising revenue you can expect to garner over the long term. It also gives you an idea of what potential similar donors are worth to your organization, informing the strategies you use to acquire, cultivate, and retain donors. It is a tool used to help shape the future of your fundraising program.

Donor lifetime value is calculated by multiplying your average donor lifespan by your gift per donor and average donor frequency. Donor lifespan is the average length of time a donor spends giving to your agency. Average gift per donor is the total amount of donations divided by the total number of donors. Donor frequency is the total number of donations made divided by the total number of donors during the same time period,

The formulas look like this:

Average donor lifespan

$$\frac{\text{Number of years you have been receiving donations}}{\text{Number of donors who have given}}$$

Average gift per donor

$$\frac{\text{Total amount of donations}}{\text{Total number of donors}}$$

Average donor frequency

$$\frac{\text{Total number of donations}}{\text{Total number of donors}}$$

Donor lifetime value

Average donor lifespan x average gift per donor x average donor frequency

Donor lifetime value is important because it gives you a baseline from which you can make budgeting decisions, allocating resources where you will receive the highest return on your fundraising investment. It will also give you a data-based foundation from which to present information to key stakeholders and board members, inform development committee and staff fundraising tasks, and increase your donor retention rate.

Developing Fundraising Processes and Procedures

Don't forget to put into place processes and procedures that reconcile the different perspectives of finance and development. You want those processes to be as easy and conflict-free as possible.

Your development team will be more focused on the different parts of external donor relationships such as raising revenues, gift structures, donor rights, and donation processes whereas finance will be more focused on internal controls, financial regulations, accounting standards, and controlling costs. Both departments are concerned with net income. Bringing their perspectives together results in reasonable revenue and cost projections without sacrificing the quality of the fundraising program.

Have your development and finance teams set financial goals, create donation processes and procedures, and draft a gift acceptance policy together. Direct them to reconcile their respective records regularly. Create an environment where all involved work to understand and respect their differences. Set up a structure where they communicate and share information regularly.

Surplus Budgeting and Wealth Building

Budgeting for a surplus makes it much more likely to happen. We talked about how to budget for a surplus in **Chapter Three**.

Building real wealth, though, involves more than realizing high positive net income. Achieving positive net income pays the bills. Building wealth provides you with freedom and control over your nonprofit's financial future.

Wealth building is the process of generating long-term income based on the acquisition of appreciating and income-producing assets. It includes savings, investments, land, and monetization of your website, to name a few.

Most nonprofits do not monetize their websites, yet they are a readily available source of income. You can monetize your website through banner ads, affiliate links, product sales, sponsorships, and memberships. Integrating ways to monetize your website is best done during the design phase.

The best way to realize positive net income is by ensuring costs are less than expenses. We talked about controlling costs in **Chapter Three**.

When you realize net surpluses, I recommend saving one-third of your surplus in reserves for unexpected emergencies, putting one-third toward investing in your staff and improving infrastructure, and investing one-third in long-term appreciating assets. Appreciating assets can take the form of an endowment, real estate, museum artifacts, or something else related to your mission that will increase in value over time and is capable of producing long-term income. It doesn't really matter the amount you set aside. If you don't like the one-third, one-third, one-third model, do something else. Just save regularly.

To minimize risk, diversify your investments. And be patient. It takes time to accumulate wealth. Slow but steady wins the race.

Planning for Mission Growth

As we have emphasized, the purpose of fundraising is to fulfill and grow your nonprofit's mission. Your individual, foundation, business, and government donors are all interested in mission attainment. As you are raising money, it is important to establish mission goals, defined here as program outreach and community support goals, as well as the financial ones.

A note of caution in formulating your mission goals. Be judicious in what gifts you accept. The last thing you want is for your mission to drift off course. Mission drift occurs when a nonprofit's resources are used for things other than mission. Yes, you need money, but not at the expense of compromising your mission.

It is easy for mission drift to occur. An opportunity to garner needed resources presents itself and the purpose of the funding is related to your mission, although not spot on. Since it will help you obtain the money you need and still partially fulfill your mission, you may elect to take advantage of the opportunity and expand your programming. Then another opportunity comes along that builds upon your expansion. And your agency has a good chance to garner the funding. The opportunity will, again, provide resources. However, this opportunity, because it is based on your expansion, may or may not promote your core mission.

> **Warning!**
>
> Be judicious in the donations you accept. Make sure they align with your mission.

Be careful. In such circumstances, your agency may or may not be prone to mission drift. Mission drift is extremely dangerous. Once mission drift begins, your organizational identity starts to change. If it continues, sooner or later donors will not know what your agency stands for, and you will lose community support. Individuals will question how their donations will be used. Foundations will not fund you because your organization is not meeting its stated mission. Businesses will see your nonprofit's weak corporate identity and not want to partner with you. Always evaluate a fundraising opportunity through the lens of core mission fulfillment.

Program Expansion

Your goal is to expand the programming that fulfills your mission. You can always partner with other community agencies to meet the needs of your clients that fall outside of your mission.

One way to expand your programming is to add services to your existing program offerings. Another way is to increase the number of people you are serving through any one program or service. In either case, you must first assess the need for the growth and whether your agency has the organizational capacity to take it on.

Before you develop new or expanded programming, determine if there is a true community need for it and make sure you have the funding in place to finance its growth. Community needs pertinent to your nonprofit's mission should be outlined in your agency's strategic plan, as should your nonprofit's current organizational capacity.

Whether you are increasing the number of programs you administer or the number of people you plan to serve, outreach is your key to success, in this case, program outreach. Which means getting the word out to the community that you are looking for clients. If you already have a pent-up demand, it will be easy to outreach to those needing your services and fill program slots. If you do not have a pent-up demand, attracting new clients will entail finding people who are interested in your services and creating demand.

Which brings us into the realm of marketing. Reaching out to those who can benefit from your services involves identifying who you want

Clarifying Point

Program outreach is a matter of describing and meeting people's needs as they define them, not just promoting your program in the community.

to serve, reaching them where they are, and making your offer attractive to them so that they consent to receive your services. In other words, targeting your market, researching them, and creating outreach materials that resonate with them such that they respond to your message. This means that a program planning or outreach team should include someone with marketing knowledge as part of the group's makeup. It's not just a matter of spreading news of your enhanced programming to the community. It's a matter of describing and meeting people's needs as they define them.

The benefit of defining needs in this way is that your requests for donations will be based on your community's needs, not your agency's need for money. Which is what motivates people to contribute. People are inspired to give by the mission you meet, not the programs you implement or money you need to implement them.

In addition, by having your outreach messages based on community input, you will hold information that can be used to develop messaging consistent with the other ways you reach out to your community, mainly through communiques about fundraising, advocacy, and voluntarism. As we saw in my companion book **The Sustainable High ROI Fundraising System**, you want one strong, consistent message to go out to your community so there is no doubt about what your organization does and the impact it makes.

Advocacy

You not only need the community to be involved with your agency's programming, you also need it to advocate for the expansion of your nonprofit's capacity. Which means that your mission must be seen as relevant by the community. Which again, puts us in the realm of marketing and crafting messages that resonate with community members. Community members who you can ask to become advocates on your behalf. Asking people to become advocates means asking them to promote your nonprofit's cause, support advancement of your agency's mission, and encourage others to join them. But first, you must create messages that they see as relevant.

Start fashioning messages that potential advocates see as germane by assessing what they currently think. Get a baseline of their perceptions. The easiest way to ask for feedback is through surveys and focus groups.

Once you have good feedback, analyze it and respond to it. You want to look at your results and ask questions like:

- What do people think we are? How do we define ourselves? Are our perceptions in sync with the community?

- What do people say about us? What is good? What is not so good?

- What results do we want to prioritize? What area for improvement do we want to tackle first?

- What positives can we build on? What are our strengths? What benefits does the community see that we offer?

- What did they say that is bad? What is the root of the problem? Can we address the root cause and change the way we do things? If we can't change things, can we turn the negative into a positive?

You now have valuable information you can use as a starting point for drafting your messages. Have your team set goals based on this information. Your overall purpose is to attract as many advocates as you can.

To entice potential advocates to interact with your organization, let them know the benefits of doing so. Make sure you tell potential supporters their investment in you is worth it, in *their* terms. To do this, determine the interests of each group you want to attract. Do some research on them. Find out what is important to and valued by

Food for Thought

Make sure you tell potential supporters their investment in you is worth it, in *their* terms.

diverse target audiences. For best results, research the perspectives of your clients, donors, board, staff, community stakeholders, and competitors.

Then look at your results in their broader context. What one overarching benefit do all the groups value about your organization? Encapsulate that in one sentence. This sentence defines the one unique benefit you bring to the community that no other nonprofit does. And that is worth advocating for.

This process enables you to use words that motivate *them*, not necessarily you and your team. Only then can you effectively portray what your nonprofit has to offer and entice potential advocates to enter into a mutually beneficial relationship with your organization.

Planning for Staff Growth

Aah. The age-old conundrum. You need more staff to meet more mission, but you need to meet more mission to raise funds to afford more staff. How do you navigate this endless cycle?

When your team sets their goals, have them account for future as well as present needs. It's not a situation of being short-staffed and having an immediate need. It's planning to be short-staffed and raising funds to meet that future need. Your development director, like you, needs to be focused on the future just as much as the present. They need to have a forward-looking orientation. Which makes creating a written strategic plan all the more important, as it is the strategic plan that depicts your organization's forthcoming state.

That's also why you want to engage in surplus budgeting and set aside a third of the surplus for future growth. So you have money to grow your staff when you need to. Your agency is not only raising money to meet current needs, but impending ones too.

And don't think it is only program staff who are important to mission fulfillment. Your core operating staff—marketing, development, IT, human resources, finance, facilities, executive management—are essential to meeting your mission too. These core operating costs are often the most difficult to raise money for. Which is why you must diversify your revenue base to focus on expanding general operating support just as much as program support. We talk at length about generating unrestricted fundraising revenues in **Chapter Six**.

Planning for Donor Growth

Planning for donor growth involves targeting and researching potential donors, designing customized communication and fundraising campaigns to reach them, and measuring the success of your results.

Target Potential Donors

Just as you target potential advocates, you target potential donors. Since it costs money to make money, you want to spend your money wisely. You don't just ask everybody to give. You ask the groups of people most likely to respond to your request. And those most likely to give have a propensity toward your cause, have the means to give, are connected to you or your nonprofit in some way, and can be reached. If any one of these conditions cannot be met, these are not your ideal donors, that is, the ones who will donate the most money with the least investment of your resources.

Research Your Targeted Donor Groups

You want to research your donors' needs, likes, preferences, and values so that they notice you, connect with you, and respond to you. I would not, at this point, research potential donors individually. I do my individual research when I am closer to making an ask. Your purpose at this stage is obtain enough information to enable you to reach a group of potential donors.

One way to identify potential donors is to calculate the donor lifetime value of your current donors, study the characteristics of the donors with the highest value, and reach out to donor groups with similar characteristics. The theory behind that approach is that your current donors are representative of your potential future donors.

You can also conduct secondary and primary research. Secondary research is information you glean from published sources such as census data, survey data, and research results. Primary research is information you glean directly from people through your observations, your survey and focus group responses, and your personal interviews. Generally speaking, secondary data is easier and less expensive to collect but primary data is more relevant. I do both if I can.

You want to gather information on things like:

- Community standard demographic characteristics (gender, age, education, income, and ethnic group)

- Community economic health and business environment

- Family makeup and activities

- Social, civic, and religious group memberships, values, and activities

- Generational group likes, preferences, values and characteristics

This is by no means an exhaustive list. The point is, you want objective data to inform your decision, not assumptions that have not been verified. You're going to spend money to reach these people. You want your information to be accurate.

Segment your potential donor list by values as much as you can. You want to establish rapport right away. People connect to other people who espouse their values. Further segment those groups by communication preferences, for example, by whether they prefer to receive email, direct mail, phone calls, or text messages. You want to reach potential donors where they are in ways that will catch and hold their attention.

Design Customized Campaigns

Design your campaigns around the likes and preferences of the different segments. Introduce your organization using the communication channels they are most comfortable with. Use the words, symbols, and images they use and respond to. Invite them to be involved in activities that they enjoy doing. To get an idea of what they will best respond to, you can look at current donors with similar characteristics and see what kinds of campaigns engage them. We talk more about asking donors to give in **Chapter Nine**.

Ensure a Positive Donor Experience

To retain the donors you worked so hard to get, you must give new donors a good experience when they interact with or make a donation to your organization. The decision tree of whether they stay or go looks something like this:

The Donor Experience

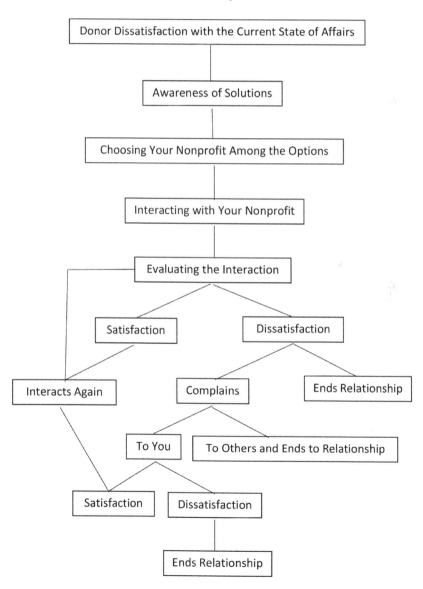

Mapping the donor journey like this and tracking conversion rates from one step to the next helps you design a user-friendly fundraising system that produces favorable results. To ensure a positive donor experience no matter who is relating to the donor, you need to establish processes and procedures that address all these points of interaction. Then you need to evaluate a sample of a string of interactions to see if the stated procedures were followed. This is especially important when working with multiple staff and/or fundraising volunteers.

When you evaluate staff or volunteer performance, take note of conversion trends. You want to do more of what encouraged a donor to move to the next step and less of what discouraged further interaction. Your objective is to uncover what techniques work best with your particular donor base and continually improve them. Also ask your donors to assess their satisfaction after their interaction. Get objective data about your and your team's performance. For best results, collect data after each interaction.

Continually test your system too. You want to make sure that each step in the process does what it is designed to do, that is, make it easy for the donor to move from one step to the next.

Measure Your Results

You will know how well you are attracting new donors by calculating your donor acquisition rate and analyzing several years' worth of trends. You want your donor acquisition rate to remain stable or increase over time. Watch your costs, though, when implementing donor acquisition efforts. It often costs more than a dollar to realize a dollar when attracting new donors. You want your donor retention rate to be much higher than your donor acquisition rate.

You will know how well you are retaining donors by calculating your donor retention rate and average donor lifespan and scrutinizing their patterns. You want both statistics to be high. To realize huge efficiencies in your fundraising activities, allocate resources to donor retention as well as donor acquisition.

Words of Wisdom

What gets measured gets done.

For an indication of your ability to realize a fundraising surplus, calculate fundraising net income. You want to see several years' worth of upward trends. If you have steady or negative trends, look at your costs and see if you can reduce them while, at the same time, striving to increase your average gift per donor.

Your average gift per donor is an indication of how effective you are in asking for money. Calculate several years' worth of information. Study your results. Ideally, your average gift per donor is increasing. If it is steady or declining, look at your costs and evaluate your processes and procedures for training your fundraising volunteers and asking for gifts.

When you look at your fundraising costs, you want to look at your cost to raise a dollar, average cost per donor, donor acquisition cost, and donor retention cost. Notice your trends and associate each rise and fall with what has happened in the external environment during the same time period. If you think costs are too high given the circumstances, you may want to cut costs or look at replacing high-cost fundraising activities with lower cost alternatives. To compare the efficiencies of different fundraising activities, calculate the return on investment for each activity. Use the data to inform your decision-making.

For a list of these and other evaluation metrics and how to compute them, see **Appendix A**.

Evaluation

Evaluation is our fifth key to financial and mission success. Evaluation provides a systematic way to study a fundraising program and determine if it reached its goals. We talked about goal setting earlier in the chapter. Conducting regular evaluation helps you understand what worked, what didn't, and why. You use evaluative data to solve problems, set new goals, budget, and benchmark and review performance. To know if your fundraising efforts are paying off, you must assess them. Plus, you want some measure of how well The Sustainable High ROI System is being implemented and performing.

The time to think about how you will assess your activities is before operations start. You want to build data collection and evaluation into your fundraising procedures before they begin so you have the information you need to measure your results after you complete each activity.

Evaluating Process

When you evaluate process, you are assessing how well your directions or procedures were followed. Assessing process tells you if your fundraising activities were implemented as intended, the barriers encountered during implementation, and what changes in procedure are needed. Process evaluation is especially important when testing a new approach, implementing a new activity, or working with other fundraising team members, particularly volunteers. For example, if your process is to follow up written requests for money to specific donors with scripted phone messages, you will want to know who each fundraising volunteer called and what roadblocks they experienced in leaving a message.

Evaluating Impact

Evaluating impact means assessing how each fundraising activity affects the overall fundraising outcome. It refers to measuring the objectives involved in achieving the outcome. You evaluate the impact of the objective whether the effect of implementing it were intended or unintended. For example, an objective for an annual appeal may be to send out x number of requests. If you send requests to people without a proclivity for your cause, you're not going to get the response you want, affecting how much money is raised and the impact of your fundraising methods.

Evaluating Outcome

Outcome evaluation is a measurement of how well you met your overall goals. It is concerned with the longer-term effects of each fundraising activity. Remember, in fundraising, outcomes are defined in terms of both mission and money. For example, a financial outcome may be "we raised x amount of dollars through our annual appeal." A corresponding donor-centric mission outcome may be "five women will sleep in safe homes tonight because of you."

Mitigating Risk

The last key to success we will discuss is mitigating risk. Don't forget about managing your risks. You never know what will happen. You need to mitigate any dangers that might harm or reduce the value of the resources you have worked so hard to acquire. Have a plan in place that protects your donor information, financial data, employee and volunteer records, and intellectual property. You want to protect against loss due to fraud, theft, and natural disaster, among other things.

You also want to protect sensitive information from being shared. I recommend you have your fundraising teams sign non-disclosure agreements (also known as confidentiality agreements) and your development staff sign non-compete agreements.

Aimee's Solution

Aimee and her board completed their strategic plan, involving the staff in formulating work objectives in line with their current capacity. The board then asked Aimee and the staff to create preliminary staffing and outreach plans to determine the costs associated with the expanding their orchestra's programming. The board also wanted an idea of how the revenues needed to fund the expansion would be raised.

Aimee assembled her teams and went to work. Teams consisted of board, staff, and volunteer representation. Each team member was chosen based on their unique expertise and perspective. The three teams were tasked with developing staffing, outreach, and fundraising plans, respectively. The purpose of the individual plans was to further the mission goals stated in the strategic plan.

To expand their donor base, they determined they needed upgraded software to more easily reach and track new donors, more hours allocated to their current 10-hour a week development director, and, with local schools interested in exposing their students to the musical arts, a new staff position—director of music education.

The fundraising team evaluated their current development efforts, establishing a baseline on which to measure progress. They looked at how much net income each fundraising activity they undertook produced. They examined the costs associated with each activity. They assessed their donor retention endeavors. They identified the characteristics of the most highly valued donors and crafted an ideal donor profile. And they looked at each fundraising activity's return on investment.

Based on their analysis of the data, the team decided to recommend changes to the current fundraising program, including a greater emphasis on the use of fundraising volunteers, dropping one of their fundraising events, continuing their grant writing endeavors, investing in hefty efforts to garner new individual donations, and beefing up their donor retention activities. Before the year was out, they started realizing more net income.

Wrapping It Up

Adopting the shared and servant leadership philosophies increases loyalty, leads to better outcomes, increases engagement, fosters respect, minimizes your workload, and enlarges your support system. To develop a shared and servant leadership culture put the needs of your organization, board members, and staff before your own interests, develop team member skills, be willing to learn from others, and encourage diversity of thought. Allow autonomy but clearly define their scope of authority. And act as a staff and board resource rather than a traditional manager.

High functioning fundraising teams create work efficiencies, improving your return on investment. When defining the purpose of your fundraising team, include the dual reason of increasing *both* funding and mission. Assemble a team with diverse experiences and complementary skills and abilities. Define organizational values and set expectations for working together. Give team members discretion over the tasks and resources needed to accomplish the group's overall purpose. Make it clear that each team member is responsible for meeting their objectives then hold them accountable for doing so. Review their progress and acknowledge their contributions regularly.

Planning for financial growth starts with an assessment of your financial needs that includes both finance and development team members. Develop processes, procedures and evaluation metrics that both meet their needs and reconciles their different perspectives. Engage in surplus budgeting. When you do realize positive net income, set aside some of the excess for operating reserves, capacity building, and investing in long-term assets. You want to build wealth as well as net income.

Before you develop new or expanded programming, determine if there is a true community need for it and make sure you have the funding in place to finance its growth. Be careful with what donations you accept, though. Stay clear of mission drift. Outreach is the key to program expansion. But it's not just a matter promoting your programs to the community. You must describe people's needs as they define them.

In addition to signing up for your agency's services, you also need community members to advocate for the expansion of your nonprofit's mission. Which means that your mission must be seen as relevant by the community. Start fashioning messages that the community can relate to by getting a baseline of their perceptions. Have your team set goals based on this information. Craft messages that let potential advocates know their investment in you is worth it.

Plan for staff growth, and their resulting expenses. Direct your team to set goals that provide for future as well as present needs. And engage in surplus budgeting. As you grow, you want enough money to seed new positions and hire the staff you need.

Planning for donor growth involves targeting potential donors, researching them, designing campaigns that will appeal to them, and measuring the effectiveness of your results. Because resources are limited, you don't go out and ask everybody to give. You ask the people most likely to respond to your request and you are likely to see a good return on your investment. One way to identify potential donors is to study your highest valued donors and reach out to donor groups with similar characteristics. You can also conduct secondary and primary research. Segment your potential donor list by values and then by communication preferences. Design customized campaigns that will reach potential donors where they are in ways that will catch and hold their attention. Make sure their experience is a satisfying one. And measure your results.

Evaluate how well your fundraising procedures were implemented, whether the process worked, and what individual elements of the plan contributed to its success or failure, and how well you met your overall goals. Build evaluation into your fundraising operations so you have the information you need to measure your results in a timely manner after each activity.

And don't forget to protect the resources you have so painstakingly gained. Make sure you manage risk.

Points to Remember

- When you combine a servant leadership philosophy with a shared leadership style, you create powerful work teams with people motivated to contribute the best they have to offer. Your board and staff work together as passionate mission ambassadors to your community increasing donations, reducing costs, and yielding a higher return on your fundraising investment.

- To build high functioning fundraising teams, define the purpose of the team, recruit diverse team members, and articulate a compelling vision. Let team members break down your vision into defined goals and tasks and set milestones to measure their progress. Give team members the tools and support they need to move forward, monitor their advancement, celebrate their successes, and reward them for their hard work.

- When your team sets goals, give them guidance on how to set SMART (specific, measurable, action-oriented, realistic, and time-bound) goals. Express your fundraising goals in financial as well as mission terms. Have them form goals and reach solutions that benefit everyone.

- The strategic plan sets direction for financial, mission, staff, and donor growth. Finance, development, program, and marketing staff must work together to create and achieve the results of their respective plans.

- Evaluation provides a systematic way to study a fundraising program and determine if it reached its goals. Conducting regular evaluation helps you understand what worked, what didn't, and why. To easily measure success, build evaluation processes into your fundraising operations.

- Mitigate dangers that might harm or reduce the value of the resources you acquire. Have a plan in place that protects your donor information, financial data, employee and volunteer records, and intellectual property and protects sensitive information from being shared.

What's Next

Now that we've laid the foundation for creating an environment conducive to effectively implementing The Sustainable High ROI Fundraising System, in the next chapter we turn our attention to the logistics of funding implementation of The High ROI Fundraising System and achieving the growth we desire.

Chapter Six

Funding The Sustainable High ROI Fundraising System Implementation

Bob, executive director of a youth services agency, was worried. With the ongoing governmental budget cuts, he was financially squeezed. There was just not enough money to hire the human resource staff he needed to recruit the qualified staff he wanted to work with the kids and families his nonprofit served. He also didn't have enough to hire more fundraisers who could raise more resources. It seemed he needed money to make money. Where was the initial investment going to come from?

The Need for Unrestricted Funding

The implementation of The Sustainable High ROI System results in work process and financial efficiencies. The money you save from these efficiencies can then be poured into further increasing your nonprofit's capacity. But you have to plan for it and go to the right places to obtain it. Where does it come from and how can you get it? For it is unrestricted money that funds core operating expansion.

Budgeting for Growth

Fundraising revenues, in most cases, are used to cover core operating expenses and any program funding shortfalls. Fundraising revenues can be restricted or unrestricted, depending on donor designations. Both are important, but undesignated donations are like gold.

If your agency is like most nonprofits, you have some funding for programs but very little for overhead. Which results in your programs growing, but not your administrative capacity. Which restricts how much mission you can meet. Which, in turn, restricts how much money you can raise. The result is that your nonprofit struggles to get ahead and is constantly under-resourced, with overworked staff.

You need to plan to get out of situations like this. You need to set financial goals and choose fundraising activities that will adequately cover both your program and core operating expenses, and then some. And you can.

What a Budget Can Look Like

Line items to include in a comprehensive expense budget may consist of:

- Personnel
- Assistance to Clients
- Program Supplies
- Software and equipment
- Telephone
- Office supplies
- Dues and subscriptions
- Staff Training
- Consultants
- Marketing
- Board Development
- Audit
- Legal fees
- Rent
- Donor Recognition
- Special Event Costs
- Operating reserves
- Budget contingencies

Your expense budget, including all these line items, might look something like this:

Expenses

Personnel

Executive Director	$ 120,000
Senior Management Team *(3 FTE)*	$ 225,000
Program Staff *(12 FTE)*	$ 480,000
Finance Staff *(3 FTE)*	$ 120,000
HR Staff *(3 FTE)*	$ 120,000
Development Staff *(3 FTE)*	$ 150,000
Administrative Staff *(3 FTE)*	$ 120,000
	$1,335,000
Fringe *(30%)*	$ 400,500
Total Personnel	$1,735,500

Non-personnel

Assistance to Clients	$ 75,000
Program supplies	$ 25,000
Software and Equipment	$ 10,000
Telephone	$ 7,500
Office Supplies	$ 12,500
Travel	$ 7,500
Dues and Subscriptions	$ 4,000
Staff Training	$ 7,500
Consultants	$ 75,000
Marketing	$ 100,000
Board Development	$ 12,500
Audit	$ 10,000
Legal Fees	$ 12,000
Rent	$ 108,000
Donor Recognition	$ 5,000
Special Event Costs	$ 15,000
Operating reserves	$ 12,000
Total Non-personnel	$ 498,500

Total Personnel and Non-personnel	$2,234,000
Budget Contingencies (5%)	$ 111,700
Total Expenses	$2,345,700

Now you know the minimum amount of money you need to raise to fully fund your level of desired growth.

Of course, as I stated in my book, ***The Sustainable High ROI Fundraising System,*** you don't base your fundraising budget on organizational budget deficits. You base your fundraising budget on your community's current economic conditions and your average rate of previous fundraising growth. You may need to adjust your organizational expense budget based on how much money you can reasonably expect to raise from your fundraising based on those conditions.

Don't set your development director up for failure. One of the top reasons fundraising staff leave their jobs is because of unrealistic expectations. You don't want to make conditions perfect for a revolving development staff door. Instead, set your staff up for success by setting reasonable goals. We talk more about retaining development staff in **Chapter Thirteen.**

Conduct a Development Cost Analysis

You must fully analyze your development costs in order to:

- Allocate your human and financial resources efficiently.

- Prioritize fundraising activities.

- Identify and eliminate fundraising activities that produce financial losses and do not promote mission.

And when you analyze fundraising costs, you analyze total costs, including personnel expenses and core operating costs allocations. When most fundraising leaders do their cost calculations, they account for direct costs only. They do not include indirect costs such as department personnel and organizational administrative allocations. But total costs tell you if the activity is producing a true net surplus rather than just funding the positions that implement them. You, as executive director, want to know and be able to substantiate that your development professionals are not net zero financial producers.

Your goal is to make money to support more than the development department. If your fundraising is only covering fundraising costs, including personnel and overhead expenses, then you need to consider implementing The Sustainable High ROI Fundraising System.

With cost information available, you can calculate not only the net income but also the return on investment of each fundraising activity you implement. That way you will be able to answer any questions from your finance committee or board that question the value of investing in certain fundraising strategies. Or why you shouldn't cut particular costs when times are economically difficult.

To perform a cost analysis, first gather information about all your costs, including direct, staff, and indirect ones. Outline all your direct expenses. Then take each staff salary and fringe and allocate costs based on the percentage of time that person spends in facilitating each activity. Don't forget about administrative time devoted to the coordination, data entry, and recordkeeping associated with each activity. Finally, allocate a portion of core operating expenses to the development department and spread those costs among fundraising activities. Add everything together and you have the true cost it takes to engage in that activity.

For example, the total costs of implementing a holiday appeal may look like this:

Direct Costs

Stationery	$ 750
Printing	$ 1,000
Postage and mailing	$ 2,500
Total direct costs	**$ 4,250**

Staff Cost Allocations

Donor Relationship Manager *(.125 FTE)*	$ 6,250
Director of Development *(.05 FTE)*	$ 3,750
Fundraising Assistant *(.125 FFTE)*	$ 5,000
Total Staff Costs	**$15,000**

Core Operating Cost Allocations (Indirect Costs)

Rent *(5%)*	$ 5,400
Telephone *(5%)*	$ 375
Office Supplies *(5%)*	$ 625
Travel	$ 75
Dues and Subscriptions *(50% Association of Fundraising Professionals dues and meetings)*	$ 360
Audit *(5%)*	$ 500
Legal Fees *(5%)*	$ 600
Total Core Operating Costs	**$ 7,935**

Total Holiday Appeal Costs	**$27,185**

What this analysis tells you is your direct mail holiday true costs are $27,185, not $4,250. And that everything the appeal brings in over $27,185 can go to supporting other core operating costs and program overages.

After the activity is completed and you have revenue numbers, you can also calculate net income and return on investment to see how well the activity performed financially.

Run your numbers. See what your projected costs are. And use the information to plan for future resource allocations.

Funding Core Operating Expenses through Fundraising

As a nonprofit, a substantial portion of your revenues must come from public support. You must reach out to your community and excite it about your mission for it to respond to your requests for money. The community you reach out to includes foundations, businesses, individuals, and governmental entities.

Funds for core costs are generally not found in foundation and government program grants and special events. Most foundation grants fund program expenses, not general and administrative ones. If they do fund general and administrative costs, it is generally a small percentage that does not come close to meeting the true need. Same with government grants. Government grants fund specific line items, usually lacking enough funding to cover all the core costs associated with administering, monitoring, and reporting on the contract. Special events, once staff time costs are accounted for, generally don't make a whole lot of money, if any, and don't produce your highest return on your fundraising dollar. On average, special events only net fifty cents on the dollar *not including labor.*

Fear not, though. Money for core operating expenses is out there. It's just a matter of tapping into it.

General Operating and Capacity Building Grants

Although there is not a lot of it since most foundation funding goes toward program support, there is a small amount of core operating funding available through grants. But, in my experience, the funding is usually very small compared to the need. And general operating grants are extremely competitive. Chances of funding are slim.

A variation of general operating grants are capacity building grants. Capacity building grants are used to grow an organization's capacity in order to meet more mission. Capacity building grants fund things like marketing studies, organizational assessments, planning activities, and consultants, to name a few. They cover some of the core operating expenses related to organizational growth. Capacity building grants are even rarer than general operating grants. And just as competitive. Like general operating grants, you can't count on getting them.

I know general operating and capacity building grants are out there. I know organizations get them. I know they're worth going for. But getting them is rare. Again and again, I see executive directors trying to cover their core operating expenses through grants. And again and again, I see them fail. Not because of lack skill or effort on the part of their grant writer. Just because raising enough unrestricted money through general operating and capacity building grants to cover all the costs is virtually impossible. There's just too much competition for not enough funds.

Yes, go for them. Just don't pin all your hopes on them.

Business Sector Contributions

According to Giving USA, business gifts account for about 5 percent of the total charitable giving in the U.S. And, unlike grants, much of it is unrestricted money. Businesses donate to nonprofits in many ways including:

- Grants
- Employee volunteer programs
- In-kind donations
- Company matching gifts
- Percentage of sales
- Sponsorships

The biggest principle to remember when you are pursuing donations from business is that you are entering into exchange relationships where both parties give and get something of value. They are two way-relationships. You get the donation, and they get a new avenue to better meet their goals. And their goals are:

- Increased visibility

- Customer acquisition

- Customer retention

- Reduced costs

You can help them meet their goals through your communications efforts, interacting with a constituency that they want to reach, associating your nonprofit's name with business endeavors, and offering employee volunteer opportunities. You can learn specifically how tap into business donations and raising big bucks in my comprehensive training **Best-Kept Secrets to Engaging and Retaining Business Donors** found at www.joanneoppeltcourses.com.

Just be careful that in going after the dollars you don't sacrifice your agency's mission or integrity. Research potential partners thoroughly to make sure their values align with yours.

Undesignated Individual Donations

Approximately 80 percent of total charitable giving in the U.S. is from individuals. According to data from Charitable Giving in the USA 2019 by CAF America, the median individual donation is around $100 while the mean is around $460. Individuals give through websites, email campaigns, direct mail campaigns, phone-a-thons, text-to-give solicitations, crowdfunding, peer-to-peer campaigns, and person-to-person meetings, among others. The top two reasons individuals give are they believe in the nonprofit's mission and that their gift will make a difference. People increase their gifts because they have more money themselves and know how previous donations were used. They are more likely to give if their contributions are matched.

Individuals are a much more stable source of funding than grants, government contracts, and special events. They don't have rigorous application requirements, onerous reporting requirements, and are generally not very labor-intensive. Individual donations, particularly email campaigns and large personal gifts, also produce a higher return on investment than other forms of fundraising. In addition, individual donors tend to give for longer periods of time than foundations or businesses.

Even though most donations are realized through individual giving and the return on investment is higher, many nonprofits spend most of their fundraising resources pursuing grants and special events. If resources are redirected, nonprofits could raise so much more. Perhaps if more nonprofit leaders understood where most of the money comes from, they would invest in fundraising strategies that attract individual donors.

General and Administrative Grant and Contract Budget Lines

If a foundation or governmental funder allows it, always include a line for general and administrative expenses in your budget. The popular percentage to use is 10 percent. However, true core operating expenses are normally between 15-25 percent, depending on the size of your agency and the amount of work volunteers perform. Although you should take advantage of general and administrative budget lines when you can, know that the amount you receive in general and administrative funds nowhere meets the actual costs.

Raising the Needed Revenues

Once you know you much money you need to raise, approach selected foundations, businesses, and individuals to raise it. Also pursue relevant government contracts to cover important agency programs. The government, though, as we stated above, does not generally fully cover all the general operating expenses associated with their contracts. You must approach foundation, businesses, and individuals to fully cover your core operating costs.

Approaching Governmental Entities

Building relationships with government funders is very different than building relationships with individuals, foundations, and corporations in that in building government relationships you have two distinct groups you need to reach: the legislators who makes the laws that provide and allocate the funding and the government employees who enforce the rules of the legislation.

Approaching Legislators

Legislators are in office because of one thing: people's votes put them there. And that is elected officials' primary objective: getting enough votes to stay in office. If you as a fundraiser want to get the attention of an elected official, talk about what's in the voters' minds, what's important to the community, and what issues are important to community voting blocks.

Ask yourself the question, who are your nonprofit's constituencies? Not only the clients, but also the supporters, like the advocates, the donors, and collaborators. How big a group are they? How influential are they? What is your reach with them? What is your influence with them? How are addressing your agency's issues important to them? How does involvement with your agency's issues affect the community and the way it votes?

You also need to talk about the mission, the public greater good. How do you talk about your mission to legislators? Do you talk about the plight of your unfortunate clients, or do you talk about the opportunity to improve the community of people who vote? Come from a position of strength, not weakness. Come from a perspective of how you can work together to address community issues that help your agency fulfill its mission and help the elected official look good in the eyes of the voters.

Elected officials also need exposure. Do you offer any fundraising or networking events where they can speak to potential voters? What about your communication channels with clients, staff, volunteers, donors, and partner agencies—can you leverage them? Do you leverage existing advocacy and communication activities as part of your government fundraising strategy? If not, you should.

Approaching Government Employees

If you are interested in a government funding opportunity, the goals of your program should be the same as those described in the legislation.

It is assumed that the legislation and the regulations surrounding it are approved by a majority of the voters through their opportunities for public comment. It is the job of the government employees to enforce the will of the people as stated in the legislation and regulations.

Government employees aren't in the game to get votes. They're in the game to carry out the purpose of the funding according to the stated rules and regulations. It's up to the government staffers to implement the program as mandated by law. If you want to get along with a government employee, know all the rules and regulations and follow them. It will make the government employee's life easier.

But knowing all the rules and regulations associated with any particular governmental funding allocation is easier said than done. First and foremost, you need to know the legislative provisions that determined the funding. And you need to know the legislation that law was built on. And the one before that. Sometimes, you need to go back to legislation that is decades old. It takes a lot of time and effort.

Then you need to know the regulations surrounding the financial and program operations of the funding. The government has particular financial and programmatic restrictions that must be followed. And your agency will, sooner or later, be audited. If you don't pass the audit, you may have return money that was already spent that you don't have. Or you may be sanctioned and subject to harsher reporting requirements. Not to mention the PR nightmares that can ensue.

So, always approach government employees with an aim toward knowing and following the rules.

Approaching Foundations

Grant funding, program and operating, most often requires researching the foundation, determining their priorities, completing the application package, and submitting the request. Sometimes, a foundation representative will also conduct a site visit or require applicants to attend in-person meetings and present before the foundation board or review committee.

You write your request to meet the expectations of those who will review your proposal. Overwhelmingly, grant reviewers are looking for mission impact. They want to fund agencies that meet the community needs they have identified. You also have reviewers who are looking for something new, something beyond the same old thing. And then there is the reviewer who is most interested in your budget, scrutinizing costs to see if they're necessary and reasonable. You have other reviewers who are most interested in your nonprofit's reputation in the community and the collaborations you have developed. To meet everyone's expectations, your request must be comprehensive. And concise.

Which is harder than it looks. Most often, funders have page, word, or character limits you must follow. Sometimes they provide you with detailed directions to guide you; sometimes, they don't. Sometimes they give you the basic structure they prefer; often, they don't. Without a defined format or with limited space, it's tough to know what information is most important to convey.

No matter what they ask for or how limited the space is, to submit a complete narrative, there are eight questions that are essential to answer in every proposal you write. The eight questions are:

1. What need will you meet?

2. How will you meet the need you describe?

3. How do you know you will be successful in doing what you say you can do?

4. How will you measure your success?

5. How much will your program cost?

6. Do you have community support?

7. How will you sustain your efforts?

8. What makes you uniquely qualified to do what you say you can do?

Answering all these questions, whether explicitly asked or not, presents a strong case for support and will ensure your proposal stands out stands out from the rest. If you're interested in learning how to answer these questions in detail, check out my training ***How to Answer***

the Eight Questions Every Grant Review Committee Asks at www. joanneoppeltcourses.com.

Approaching Businesses

The first step in garnering support from businesses is making them aware of your nonprofit's existence. You can do this in a number of ways including networking with businesses at their events; participating in business association workgroups; guesting on business-focused radio and TV programs; advertising in business publications; submitting articles to business-directed magazines, newspapers, and other publications; and sponsoring a business event. You can also design your website so that it contains keywords that business professionals may use in an internet search. You have to pursue them, though, Otherwise, you won't get their attention.

To connect with business professionals so they easily understand you, use common business terms. Be familiar with the terms brand, brand awareness, market demand, market penetration, value proposition, unique marketing position, customer journey, and customer experience.

When you describe the impact your nonprofit makes in the community, you want to talk in terms of business measures of performance, including both mission and money. Common measures of market performance include the number of clients you serve; number of community event invitees and attendees; number of social media likes, followers, and number of engagements; number of website visitors; number of unique website visitors; number of people on your mail and email lists; frequency of contact; and email open and click through rates. If you're going to post flyers, let them know how many you will print, where you'll post, and how often you will replenish the supply.

Common measures of financial performance include net income, assets, net assets, receivables, liabilities, liquidity, and debt ratios. Although knowing the ins and outs of financial statements is out of the realm of fundraising, it is imperative that you understand how to read and interpret a basic audit and 990 and that you understand your nonprofit's general financial position.

When you get down to talking about financial partnerships, know the approximate value of what you're offering. Research industry benchmarks. Come from a position of strength.

As you continue the conversation, make sure you specify and clarify details. Ask them, "Here is what I have to offer—what works best for you?" Talk about expectations on both sides regarding your respective communication processes and implementation procedures, as well as the deliverables you both promise.

Prepare a written agreement that you both sign. Memorialize what you agree to in writing. The amount of money involved and the complexity of the arrangement will determine whether you present a simple memorandum of understanding or an attorney-prepared a contract.

Then do what you say you're going to do. Live up to your end of the bargain. And communicate with them about your progress. Make it easy to for them to say yes to you if you ask them for a donation again.

Approaching Individuals

A donor needs four things to give to your nonprofit: awareness of your agency, a way to donate, the ability to give, and investment in your organization. Most people don't give large donations without a relationship in which to do it. The first phase of acquiring new donors is to identify them. The second phase is to develop a relationship with them. Then, when the timing is right, you ask for money.

So, how do you attract support for your cause?

Engage in comprehensive planning. Plan your strategy and how you will measure your results. What gets measured gets done. Use your strategic plan as a guide to create your development plan. To keep your fundraising aligned with your nonprofit's mission, your development plan should be an outcrop of your strategic plan.

Stay mission focused. It is mission that motivates, not a need for money. Donors want to impact a cause, not balance a checkbook. Talk about forwarding the mission when you talk to donors, not the money you need to run a program.

<table>
<tr><td>

Clarifying Point

Always put mission first. Always.

</td></tr>
</table>

People are driven by values, feelings, and beliefs. They want to be acknowledged and validated. And they want to be part of something bigger than themselves. Appeal to their underlying values, feelings, and beliefs in your asks. Answer the questions, "How will I contribute to the greater good by giving to you? What part of being successful can I be? What will I get that is important to me if I give to you?"

Donor research is key. Know your donors' values, preferences, and motivations so you can speak to their underlying needs. Know donors' perspectives and experiences. Your goal is to attract more individuals to support your cause. And the surest way to do that is by replicating the kind of donors you already have. We talked about the benefits of attracting like-minded donors in **Chapter Five**.

Look at your agency's existing connections. Recruit from among your existing base of businesses—your board, staff, vendors, advocates, former clients, and current clients. They are already familiar with your nonprofit and, in one way or another, vested in its success. Ask them to be part of making that success happen.

When you are in search of new donors, don't just go after anyone or appeal to the general public. Try and connect with those people who will take the time to notice you and be most likely to respond to your message. Use resources where they have the greatest chance of producing the highest returns. To spread awareness, target your audiences.

Survey your existing and potential supporters. Asking donors for their opinions validates them. When asked for their opinions or advice, people feel important, that they matter, and that their voice counts. Listen to what your donors say is important to them. Analyze their responses to see what they are telling you about the quality of their relationship with your nonprofit. Ask yourself, how can you make it easier for them, both in terms of motivation and process, to interact with you so their needs are met, they support your organization, and more mission is fulfilled?

Be very, very clear in your call to action. Be direct and be specific. And give a deadline. Make sure there is no doubt about what you want them to do.

Follow up on any request you make. When people respond to you, reply back. Show them you know and appreciate what they did. Thank them and give them feedback on the results of their actions. Let them see how crucial they are to making a difference in their community. Then engage them some more. Send them another call to action. Create an ongoing positive cycle of donor engagement and mission fulfillment.

Don't make all your requests about donating money. Donors are turned off when they hear from you only when your agency needs money. It's not only them giving to you, but also you giving to them. If you want them to respond to you, you need to respond to them. If you want them to meet your needs, meet theirs first. Send them messages using communication channels they are most comfortable with. Show them you know and respect their values and preferences.

Value annual gifts as much as large, structured gifts. There is no reason a wealthy donor cannot structure his or her gift to benefit both the here and the now as well as the future. You can arrange a situation where your nonprofit sees both annual payouts and a large future gift while the donor realizes maximum tax benefits. You can talk to a financial advisor or estate attorney to learn about all the options available.

Bob's Solution

Bob decided to first analyze his program and fundraising costs. He wanted to see how much he really needed to raise to cover the program costs that were losing funding and still reach a net surplus. Once he had a good handle on his total program costs, he could align his fundraising and mission needs. Once he had a good handle on each of his fundraising activity costs, he would be able to work with his development director to set data-driven financial goals, rather than the 5 percent increase he currently budgeted. He could redirect his staff to focus on fundraising activities that produced the most net income with the least amount of resources. Armed with that information, he would also be able to speak to board members' concerns about his plan for dealing with the revenue cuts.

In addition, he decided to focus staff time toward attaining more individual donations and reduce the number of special events the agency held. His costs analysis showed him that his three events, once labor and overhead expenses were factored in, did not make any money. He would talk to his development director about what one event promoted the most mission and brought them the greatest amount of community visibility. He would scrap the other two events.

With more time at her disposal, the grant writer had more time to pursue general operating grants and the development director had more time to court businesses and cultivate individual donors for large personal gifts. More general operating revenues began to roll in,

With the resource reallocation and increased revenue, within six months, the agency was realizing a net surplus, much of it in unrestricted income. Bob was able to invest in the human resource staff he needed to recruit the qualified program staff he wanted. At the end of two years, he was also able to raise base salaries. Within five years, operating reserves doubled, and the board added to the organization's endowment.

Wrapping It Up

If your agency is like most nonprofits, you have funding for programs but not overhead. You need to plan, through your budgeting, to rectify situations like this. Budget for the things you need to grow, just as much as direct and indirect expenses. Then you know the minimum amount of money you need to raise to fully fund your level of desired growth. Once you know you much money you need to raise, you will approach foundations, businesses, and individuals to raise it.

Fully analyze your development costs in order to allocate resources more efficiently, prioritize fundraising activities, and eliminate workload that produces a financial loss and does not promote mission. To perform a cost analysis, gather total cost information, outline direct expenses, allocate personnel costs based on the percentage of time spent in facilitating each activity, allocate a portion of core operating expenses to each fundraising activity, and add everything together.

Funds for core costs are generally not found in foundation and government program grants and special events. There is a small amount of general operating funding available through foundation operating grants, However, general operating and capacity building grants are extremely competitive.

Business donations are another source of core operating funding. According to Giving USA, corporate contributions make up 5 percent of total charitable giving in the U.S. Just be careful you don't sacrifice your agency's mission or integrity in pursuit of the dollars. Also, thoroughly research potential partners to make sure their values align with yours.

Individuals are the most plentiful sources of core operating funding. Approximately 80 percent of total charitable giving in the U.S. is from individuals. Individuals are a much more stable source of funding than grants, government contracts, and special events, tending to give for longer periods of time than foundations or businesses without the onerous reporting requirements of government contracts. And the return on investment for individual donations tends to much higher than other forms of giving.

Points to Remember

- If you want your agency to grow financially, include line items for operating reserves and budget contingencies. And when you analyze a fundraising activity's cost, analyze total costs, including personnel expenses and core operating cost allocations. Analyzing total costs tell you if the activity is producing a true net surplus and helps you allocate resources more effectively.

- General operating grants are few and far between, making them extremely competitive. No matter what they ask for or how limited the space is, a complete grant narrative addresses community need, process to meet that need, a definition and measurements of success, costs to implement your intervention, the level of community support your nonprofit and cause enjoy, sustainability, and organizational uniqueness.

• The biggest principle to remember when you are pursuing donations from business is that you are entering into exchange relationships where both parties give and get something of value. When you approach businesses, speak their language and address their priorities. Come from a position of strength, knowing your nonprofit's value in business terms. Talk about expectations, be specific, and put agreements in writing. Live up to your end of the bargain, communicating your progress along the way.

• Approximately 80 percent of total charitable giving in the U.S. is from individuals. Identify them, get their attention, build a relationship with them, engage them in the work of your nonprofit, and then, when the timing is right, ask them for a donation.

What's Next

When you begin implementing The Sustainable High ROI System and reaching out to foundations, businesses, and individuals for funding, you want to keep track of not only your revenues and expenses, but other data that you can use to substantiate success as well. In the next chapter, we address the types of data you want to collect, your ensuing software needs, and how to utilize all that data to your advantage.

Chapter Seven

Collecting and Using Data

al was working on her museum's budget. She was planning an increase to the salary line. It was time to add another fundraising position. Val knew the first question finance committee members would ask. "How much will that improve our fundraising results?"

Val thought about the added costs and pondered how she would structure her development department's time. She knew she needed to prove a high return on investment. And she knew she had about six months to do it. "Good," she thought. Enough time to track and analyze data.

First, she needed to evaluate financial performance and compare it to industry benchmarks. She wanted committee members to know how well the agency was performing in relation to others.

Next, she needed to analyze how her development director was currently spending her time. Val wanted to know how she could leverage what the development director was already doing with any new initiatives the added staff undertook. What activities resulted in the most net income? What about visibility? New donors? What information would best help Val convince her finance committee to support the investment in fundraising?

The Importance of Collecting Data

As we talked about in **Chapter Five**, one of the keys to successfully implementing The Sustainable High ROI Fundraising System is evaluation.

You need to measure your progress in meeting whatever goals you have set. If you don't, you'll never know if you got where you wanted to go. And you will never be able to communicate success to others—an important component in exciting your community and engaging your board.

You collect data about your board, staff, and community. It is much easier to collect the data produced by a series of actions as you go along rather than long after the actions have been completed when memories have become fuzzy, and people have moved on. You need to build organizational processes and procedures for gathering needed data into your operation as key components of your Sustainable High ROI Fundraising System, rather than thinking of evaluation as something that is tacked on at the end.

So, determine what data you and your board need to evaluate progress and build the collection of that data into your operations. When you design your implementation tactics, do it with evaluation metrics and processes in mind.

Kinds of Data to Collect

Collecting fundraising, marketing, and financial data and analyzing the metrics can help you budget realistically, make resource allocation decisions, set and meet fundraising goals, benchmark performance, evaluate results, and formulate solutions when outcomes are less than optimal. Further, the objectivity intrinsic to numerical measurements supports data-based decision-making. Data-based decisions exude credibility, enhancing your position as leader of your agency.

The fundraising data you will need to track includes, at a minimum:

- Fundraising goals
- Donor contact information
- Donor types (individual, foundation, business, etc.)
- Donation dates
- Donation amounts
- Gift method (check, credit card, stock, real estate, etc.)

- Asking method (personal solicitation, direct mail, email, phone, etc.)
- Event attendances

In addition to fundraising data, to conduct a thorough review of your fundraising effectiveness, you need marketing data. You will gather marketing statistics from Google Analytics or other tracking software, your email provider, and your social media platform. Marketing information to gather includes:

- Website visitor types (unique, organic, paid, etc.)
- Landing page visits
- Time on website pages
- Emails sent by campaign
- Email open rates
- Email click through rates
- Email bounce rates
- Email response rates
- Social media followers by channel
- Social media postings by channel
- Dates of social media postings
- Social media likes by posting
- Social media shares by posting
- Responses to questionnaires and surveys
- Conversion rates

The end goal is to analyze how your marketing and fundraising endeavors affected your financial results. You are trying to raise money, after all. You will assemble financial data from your nonprofit's financial records, such as budgets, audits, and 990s. Important financial figures related to fundraising to assemble include:

- Fundraising revenues by campaign
- Donor recruitment expenses
- Fundraising costs by campaign by line item
- Development department direct costs by line item
- Development department indirect costs by line item

Software Needs

Invest in the most robust technology you can afford that will effectively track the information you need and monitor trends. You will want to monitor both fundraising and marketing performance. You may want to look at systems that integrate the collection and analysis of fundraising and marketing information.

There are hundreds of software management systems on the market at all price levels. Ask for demonstrations from the software companies you are considering and talk to other users to find the right program for you.

When comparing costs, check how much they charge to convert your current data into the new system. And expect fundraising expansion. You want a software package that can grow with your fundraising program.

When choosing fundraising software, make sure it:

- Is easy to understand how and where to enter data. As you grow, you may have multiple users entering data, and you want the entries to be uniform.

- Has a place to enter your fundraising goals. You want to be able to compare this year's goals to this year's performance and this year's performance to last year's performance.

- Allows you to analyze the performance of individual fundraising activities as well the four fundraising channels—individual donations, foundation giving, corporate contributions, and government contracts. You want to know what activities are performing best and who is responding to them.

- Contains enough space for multiple years of notes in a donor's profile.

- Has mail merge capabilities that can personalize the name, address, last donation amount, and this year's requested donation amount. Personalized appeals always perform better than impersonal ones.

- Can run donor and donation reports, including donor history, average gift per donor, donation growth, donor acquisition, and donor retention rates. You will want to be able to track what's going on year to date, compare year over year, and see trends.

- Tracks who entered what data, when. You want to be able to go back if you have questions or supervise someone who is doing the data input.

Utilizing Your Data

Put procedures into place that ensures data entry is accurate and stays current. You need your reports to accurately reflect what is happening at your agency so you and your board can make good decisions regarding the future. Base decision-making on objective data instead of what you or board members think or feel. It is less risky than following an idea that has no basis in facts.

Use your data to see where you can implement interventions that will increase your return on your investment and magnify your mission impact. Your all-important goal is to achieve the highest results with the least drain on resources. You want to grow your fundraising program and increase net income to build your nonprofit's capacity to meet more mission. You want a sustainable "more mission—more money—more mission—more money" cycle to take hold.

Warning!

Never base projections or evaluations of fundraising results on revenues alone. It's not gross income that counts—it's net income. Your most useful financial ratios will account for your total fundraising costs.

When you report fundraising results, don't fall into the trap of reporting gross instead of net income. Although your gross numbers sound more impressive, they don't give you all the information you need to truly assess financial performance. And when you calculate net income, account for your total fundraising costs, not just your direct ones. Again, the numbers will not be as impressive, but you and your board will have more accurate information on which to assess past performance and influence future direction.

Use your data to benchmark your organization's fundraising performance. Calculate the metrics we outlined in **Chapter Three** and create realistic fundraising goals based on the ratio of revenue to costs. See what fundraising activities give you the biggest bang for your buck.

When you examine fundraising reports, in addition to net income, look at average gift per donor, donor acquisition, and donor retention rates. Study your trends. You want to examine year-to-date comparisons to see how you are progressing toward your goal and adjust as necessary. You can go back even further, say five years, to analyze long-term trends. Long-term trends help you see your rate of growth over time. Use the average annual growth rate to forecast your upcoming year's rate of expansion. Often, the best predictor of future performance is past results.

And if you notice substantial deviation in your trends, note why. For example, a change in executive directors often leads to poorer fundraising results. Or a recession hits and affects your donors' ability to give. Or you have a fire, or a pandemic hits and operations shut down. You want to know what circumstances or interventions caused the deviations, good or bad. You want to plan better for the next time there is an unexpected change in circumstances. You also want to know what actions to continue or discontinue so that you realize maximum positive fundraising results going forward. Use the data and tools available to you to knock your fundraising results out of the park.

You also want to associate your marketing activities and fundraising performance. You want to see if and how strong the relationship is between the two. Marketing generally enhances fundraising. Leverage scarce resources, reduce organizational costs, and magnify outcomes by intertwining your fundraising efforts with your agency's marketing campaigns.

For further discussion, see the ***Nonprofit Quick Guide: Raising Lots of Money: Essential Measures to Grow Your Finances and Excel at Fundraising.***

Val's Solution

Val's development director started gathering more detailed marketing, fundraising, and financial data. Val and her development director worked together to create data collection processes and procedures that easily integrated with other organizational systems, such as finance and human resources. They also developed regular reports that would be easy for finance and development committee members to digest and the board as a whole to understand.

The reports were received well. The development committee had objective evidence that what they were doing was working. The finance committee had the cost data it needed to budget effectively. And board and staff had the information they needed to set realistic fundraising goals and evaluate results.

The increase in the budget was approved, though not at the level Val had hoped. Still, Val knew that as her staff continued to collect information and she could show progress in meeting their goals, the board would again invest in fundraising staff growth.

Wrapping It Up

Marketing enhances fundraising which leads to revenue generation. To efficiently increase net income and improve return on investment, you need to measure your organization's progress in meeting the fundraising, marketing, and financial goals you have set. You must be able to communicate progress to your community if you want the big donations.

So that you have accurate and current information, build data collection processes and procedures into your program design. When you compute your financial ratios, make sure to account for costs and apply total, not just direct, costs to your calculations. And look at trends, analyzing several years' worth of information. Use the numbers to benchmark fundraising performance, direct efforts to increase your return on investment, and analyze the relationship between your fundraising and marketing efforts. Let the data inform your plans and suggest adjustment to your plans when fundraising is not going as well as expected.

Points to Remember

- Prepare for fundraising growth. Purchase the most robust technology you can afford to track statistics and monitor trends. Explore fundraising and marketing software packages that can handle organizational expansion.

- Make sure your data entry is accurate and current. You need up-to-date information that truly reflects where your nonprofit stands so you and your board can make solid plans that improve your fundraising results.

- Data-based decisions are less risky than those not grounded in the facts. The objectivity inherent in data-based decision-making establishes a concrete foundation for your leadership and conveys impartiality when evaluating performance.

What's Next

With data-based goals and objectives on which to measure your progress toward putting The Sustainable High ROI Fundraising System into operation, you are ready to go out and start raising money.

I know the most comfortable asks are arms-length asks rather than in-person solicitations. Approaching potential donors via grants and special events is not a heavy personal emotional lift. But approximately 80 percent of the charitable giving pie is from individuals. Person-to-person solicitation is also the most cost-effective way to raise money, producing a very high return on your fundraising investment. As such, we now turn our attention to quelling the fears most of us have around asking individuals for money.

Chapter Eight

Taming Your Fundraising Fears

Lydia's stomach was churning. She hated this part of being an executive director—asking people for money. Yet it had to be done. Her legal services agency couldn't survive without the influx of outside funds. She sighed as she fretted about the upcoming lunch meeting she had with the Davis'. How would she ever get through this?

How to Get Comfortable Talking about Money with Donors

Many of us have grown up learning not to talk about money. We were taught money was a taboo subject, especially asking someone else about their personal finances. So, when it comes to asking for money, we are necessarily uncomfortable. And big time squeamish when we have to meet with donors. How can we help calm our fears and fearlessly talk to others about money?

Remember the goal of The Sustainable High ROI Fundraising is to raise money to support your mission. The end goal is mission advancement, not money for money's sake. So, when you meet with donors, take the focus off money you want to raise and onto the impact your nonprofit makes. Instead of framing the conversation around money, frame it around your agency's mission and your passion for it. Focus on telling your story: why you got involved, why you stay involved, and why you increased your involvement. Let your eyes shine with excitement. Then invite them to share their story with you.

Another practice that makes it more comfortable to talk about money is to keep your eye on the prize. Dream about how many lives your organization can change. Think about the impact you and your donors have made so far and how much more your organization can accomplish with more people on board. Ask the person to whom you're talking to join you on the road to success.

How to Overcome Your Fear of Asking

Eventually, though, you come to a point in the conversation when it's time to ask for a donation. And that point in time may be scary. How do you overcome your fears?

Acknowledge and face your feelings. When you label your emotions and allow yourself to express them, they become manageable. You feel a greater sense of control and power. Use those feelings of power and control to your advantage.

You can also reframe your feelings, viewing your nervousness as your mind's way of revving you up for the situation. The adrenaline rush can be seen as either positive or negative. See it as positive.

If you are intimidated, it is important to view the donor as a human who engages in the same daily personal care tasks that you do. Put the person on an even footing with you. See them as your equal.

Preparation helps too. Don't go in by the seat of your pants. Do your research. Get to know your donors. Make them more familiar than unknown.

If you fear the worst, challenge your thoughts. Ask yourself how likely it is that whatever terrible situation you're thinking of will happen. Is what you're imagining a rational thought? If it is, what's the worst result that can happen? They say, "No?" If they do say no, you're not going to be any worse off than you are now. Can you handle that?

How to Look Calm When You Are Stressed

Of course, your anxiety may still pop up. To help avoid that, engage in self-care: get enough sleep, exercise, and eat healthy foods. Good health will help you maintain a more relaxed state of mind.

Be prepared for your meeting. Practice your pitch. Become familiar with your words so that delivering them is second nature and feels normal. Don't let your own words stress you out.

Before you go into an important donor meeting, de-stress. Listen to music, get some fresh air, or let your thoughts flow and write about the upcoming encounter. Research has shown that doing one or more of these things will reduce your stress level.

Deep breathing is one of the most effective methods for reducing edginess. When you feel yourself tensing up, take a few deep breaths in and out and then breathe normally. The deep breaths will help calm you and slow you down.

You can also engage in stress-relief exercises, relaxing the all the muscles in your body. One practice I have found helpful is to tense my muscles for 10 seconds, close my eyes, take deep breaths, and then concentrate on relaxing single muscle groups one at a time until I am fully relaxed.

Another practice that may help you loosen up is to visualize yourself as calm. See yourself as you want to be in your mind's eye. Impress your brain with your desired self-image. Let positive thoughts lead your thinking.

To be perceived as comfortable during the conversation, sit up straight but not too rigidly. Drop your shoulders. Don't tap your foot or wring your hands. Speak slowly and maintain eye contact. Focus on the speaker, not yourself.

If you do tense up while you're talking, ask a question. Put the focus on them, taking it off you and giving you time to recoup and relax.

Finally, be yourself. Know that you're okay just the way you are. Above all, people appreciate honest, genuine interactions. And you do that by being you.

Lydia's Solution

Lydia took a few deep breaths. She decided she would go for a short walk around the block before she left for lunch. While on her walk, she started to analyze her situation. How prepared for the conversation was she? Pretty prepared, she thought. She had done her research and had an idea of the Davis' capacity to give what she was going to ask from them. She knew some of the other causes they gave to. She wasn't relying on a wish or hunch. She knew her stuff.

She also thought about the worst that could happen. The worst that could happen is they would say no. If that happened, no harm, no foul. The ensuing ask really wasn't much of a risk.

She headed to her car and got in. As she was driving, she went over some of the questions she wanted to ask. And visualized getting engaged responses. She pictured the meeting going well and smiled. She was going to be okay.

Wrapping It Up

To feel comfortable talking to donors about money, frame the conversation around your agency's mission, focus on the impact your nonprofit makes in the community, and tell the story of why you got involved, why you stay involved, and why you increased your involvement. Think about the impact a donation would make and ask the donor to join you on the road to success.

To overcome your fears about asking for money, acknowledge and face your feelings and view your nervousness as your mind's way of revving you up for the situation. See the donor as the same human you are, putting them on equal footing with you. Be prepared by doing your research. And if you fear the worst, challenge your thoughts, asking yourself how likely what you're thinking will happen and what's the worst if it does.

There are a number of things you can do to look and be calm during your conversations with donors. Practice your ask beforehand. De-stress by listening to music, getting some fresh air, or writing your thoughts down. Practice deep breathing. Tense and relax the muscles in your body. Visualize yourself as calm. Watch your body posture. Ask questions. And be yourself.

Points to Remember

- To avoid stressing out, take care of yourself—exercise, eat healthy foods, and get plenty of sleep.
- When you speak to a donor, sit up straight, speak slowly, and maintain eye contact.
- To shift the focus from you to them, ask questions.

What's Next

Not only do you need to feel and look comfortable during conversations with donors, you must also ask for what you want. The next chapter focuses on how to solicit the donation—the culmination of exciting your community, which is step three of The Sustainable High ROI System.

Chapter Nine

The Complete Guide to Asking

Frank, the executive director of a county-wide disabilities agency, needed a sustainable influx of unrestricted dollars to supplement the decreasing government funding his nonprofit was receiving. He also wanted to cover some of the costs his clients had no resources for, such as hobbies and trips.

Frank knew general operating grants wouldn't cover all his needs, nor were they long-term sources of revenue. And he had already started a corporate giving program. To generate even more revenue, he pondered asking people of wealth for large personal gifts. Who did he know that he could approach?

He thought of Linda, whose husband was the executive vice president of worldwide operations at a Fortune 500 company. He had met Linda in a social setting and she had come to two of his agency's community awareness fundraisers. He also knew she had a cousin she was close to with special needs. Perhaps she would be interested in making a donation. But he was not very experienced in asking people for substantial sums of money. He hoped he would get a positive reception.

Asking Techniques that Guarantee a Positive Reception

Step three of The Sustainable High ROI System is to excite your community so that it eagerly supports your agency. You excite community members about your cause through targeting, branding, and spreading your unique marketing position, which we talked about at length in my book *The Sustainable High ROI Fundraising System.*

Exciting people about your cause means you focus on mission, not finances, when talking with them, the same mindset you take to calm your fears about making the ask. Making it about mission not only sets off your passion, it also sets off your potential donor's. When you make the ask, introduce your agency as one of most effective ways they can forward the cause they care about. Then you proceed by asking for a donation. But just how do you ensure your ask is well received?

Form a Relationship First

You approach those with the greatest propensity to give, those who have an interest in your cause. And you do that within the context of a relationship.

Your Approach

Your first approach is not an ask for money. How would you react if someone came up to you and said, "Hi, my name is Joanne. Will you donate x amount of dollars to my nonprofit?"

While a few persons may give you money if you approach them that abruptly, you'll alienate most people. And then word of mouth starts to spread, and your agency gets a reputation for always having its hand out. And then it becomes harder to excite your community. No, it's not a good idea to approach people with an ask for money. Develop a relationship first.

The goal of your initial conversation is to connect, find information, and get a better understanding of one another. Then you build a relationship based on trust, respect, and mutual interest in your organization—and not because you want to get money out of them.

People do not like to be treated as cash machines. The end goal of a potential donor is not to balance a checkbook. The end goal of a donor is to make a positive impact on an issue they care about. They want to be acknowledged and valued for their contributions, not how much money they have.

Food for Thought

Would you rather have donors that talk about your organization's need for money or talk about your mission and the impact your agency makes, spreading the good news to others, exciting the community for you?

Plus, there are things other than money you want of potential donors. For example, you want donors to say good things about your nonprofit. You want advocates for your cause. Would you rather have donors that talk about your organization's need for money or talk about your mission and the impact your agency makes, spreading the good news to others, exciting the community for you?

Then don't start a relationship based on money. Talk to them about their dreams of making an impact. Build a satisfying relationship with them. Acknowledge and value them for who they are, not what they have.

Questions to Ask

A good starting point is to ask questions. Find out more about them. Give them an opportunity to feel understood and accepted. Validate them. Let them know you want to enter into a relationship with them, no matter what the outcome.

And talk about yourself too. Be authentic. Authenticity is about being about open, honest, and vulnerable. Most people will respond in kind. Most people want to be in community with others.

Questions you can ask include:

- What is most important to you?
- What is not important to you?
- What are you grateful for?
- What is your ideal state of being?
- What are some of your goals for next year?
- What kind of change do you want to see?
- What is one of the best gifts you can give your community?

- If you were in charge, what would you do differently than is being done now?

- If money was not an issue, what is the one thing you would do for your community?

- How do you see us working together to meet our respective goals?

- What can I do to deepen your trust in our organization?

Connect on Values

Asking the questions I postulated above will give you insight into what your potential donor's values are, where you can connect with them at a very deep level. Connecting with people on values builds camaraderie and a shared interest in success. That's a great foundation on which to build a donor relationship.

People act in accordance with their values. Our values determine what we consider important in the way we live and work. Living our values is how we achieve purpose. They mold our priorities and drive our behaviors. They help us create the future we want to experience.

How people allocate and spend money is an expression of their values. People devote time and money to endeavors that are important to them and give them purpose. That's why we contribute and volunteer to causes we care about—they make life worth living for us. We feel a great sense of fulfillment when we act upon and live according to our values.

What values does your nonprofit hold? Do you have a values statement? Talking about organizational values will help attract donors who cherish the same things you do. Which means you can ask what fulfilling their values is worth to them. See how the conversation is not, then, about money? Money is just an expression of their values.

And since you are both trying to accomplish the same thing, you share goals. And reaching goals together creates a sense of teamwork and belonging. And reaching milestones in your journey together leads to a sense of accomplishment and purpose. Which reinforces the pursuit of values. Which improves loyalty. All things you want from a potential donor.

There are many benefits to connecting on values. Get at the values first, before asking for money.

Listen More Than You Talk

People love to talk about themselves. And people love to give advice. So let them. Ask them questions and listen to their responses. In addition to learning about them, their values, and priorities, it puts the focus on them instead of you, giving you time to breathe and relax, as we talked about in **Chapter Eight**.

When you listen, actively listen. Active listening involves paying attention to both verbal and nonverbal cues and confirming your interpretation of the messages you receive. Be attuned to and reflect feelings as well as facts. Your goal is to come to a mutual understanding between you and the potential donor, on both an emotional and rational level.

Active listening is something you are wholly involved in and fully present for. You must be attentive to the speaker, not planning on what you're going to say next, judging or interrupting them, jumping to conclusions, or imposing your opinions or solutions. You empathize and validate without necessarily agreeing. "I understand" are great words to use.

To show you are listening to them, face the speaker and maintain eye contact. Focus entirely on what they are saying. Give them 100 percent of your attention.

To get the other person talking to you, ask open-ended questions. The ones stated earlier are a good start. Paraphrase what you heard. At the end of the conversation, summarize what you heard and clarify next steps.

Acknowledge and Validate

We are social creatures and have a basic need for social interaction. We thrive when we are an accepted part of a community, being drawn to people who approve or agree with what we think, say, or do. We all need to be acknowledged and valued for who we are. That is part of being human. Tell people that you value them. Acknowledge and validate them.

You let people know you value them when you listen to them. You are giving your time to hear what they have to say. You acknowledge people's importance by asking about their lives and being interested in their situations. All that active listening does more than uncover information. It helps the person on the other end see that you care about them.

As a nonprofit leader, you want potential donors to feel good about future involvement with your agency. As a potential donor, you want confirmation that you are making a good decision and doing the right thing. You want to know that you matter, that your donation will make a difference. If I, in my role as fundraiser, can do that for you, you are more likely to donate to my cause.

> **Clarifying Point**
>
> You acknowledge people's importance by asking about their lives and being interested in their situations.

Not that you approach potential donors with an end goal to get money out of them. No. As we learned earlier in the chapter, the goal of your initial interaction is to connect, uncover information, and gain a clearer understanding of one another. And out of that you build a relationship that advances the mission of your organization. Just let people know they are an important part of making the mission happen. Acknowledge and validate their participation.

When You Ask

When you do ask them for money, be clear. Don't ask them to complete two or more actions or give them choices. Ask them to do one thing—make a donation.

Be brief. Don't drone on and on. Get down to the point. If you've been steering the conversation toward meeting mutual goals that fulfill their values and have validated their involvement, they won't be surprised when you turn the conversation to financing your efforts. It will be a natural outcrop. Don't hide the discussion around money with superfluous words. Be brief and concise.

Ask for a specific amount, for something in the range of x amount.

And then be quiet and don't say anything. Let them think. Let them be the first to break the silence. I know the silence is uncomfortable. Let it be until they respond. The ball is in their court. Don't take it away from them. Let them pick it up and throw it back to you.

After You Ask

After every interaction, especially after promise of a donation, express lots of gratitude. A simple thank you goes a long way toward building strong donor relationships. Saying thank you acknowledges and validates the actions of someone who has gone out of their way to make a donation. Saying thank you meets your donor's basic need to feel appreciated. And people welcome having their needs met. People are much more likely to respond to your needs if you respond to theirs.

To create the most effective donor relationships, thank your donors not only when they donate, but whenever they respond to a call to action. You can never thank your donors too often. I have never met any donor who was offended by being thanked too much unless the thank you came across as unauthentic. Let your donors know you know and cherish what they did. Thank them each time they contribute to your mission, whether it be time, talent, or treasure. Meet their emotional needs. Keep building that goodwill. Then engage them some more. Send them another call to action. Create an ongoing positive cycle of donor engagement and mission fulfillment.

Since the donor has given, you know they are invested enough in your agency's mission to donate. Build on that emotional investment. Take the next step to developing a successful relationship and ask your donor to do something other than donating. Ask them to follow you on Facebook, take a survey, join you for an educational event— whatever it is, engage them. Increase the likelihood that you will retain your donors and they will give again. And keep thanking them. It all starts with that first thank you.

Uncovering Capacity to Give

Now that you know how to ask, how do you know how much to ask for? Well, you do your research. And you do two types of research: secondary research and primary research. You need both.

Secondary research is information you find through published sources, like the internet, wealth screening software, or public records. You want to at least Google the person to see what you can find. Wealth screening software will also give you an idea of the person's net worth, give you access to information you may not find on your own, and save you time in other types of research.

If you don't have wealth screening software, however, don't worry. Whatever information you glean from secondary research should be confirmed through primary research anyway. Direct personal research always outperforms secondary research. If you have only a handful of potential donors of wealth, the investment in the screening software won't be worth it. I have worked with plenty of nonprofits that do not have wealth screening software and still get large donations.

Primary research is research you gain from people themselves. You can conduct one-on-one interviews, focus groups, surveys, or observations. Because of the sensitivity of the information and the fact that it is the most effective way to realize a donation, you will want to engage in a one-on-one interaction. Which means being observant and asking your potential donors questions directly.

Indicators of Individual Donor Capacity

Observation is one way to assess the outward indicators of wealth. Being observant means looking at the kind of car they drive, the clothes they wear, or the neighborhoods they live in. But there are plenty of people of wealth who live modestly and there are plenty of people who look wealthy that are living beyond their means. The trappings of wealth or lack thereof are not always a good indicator of capacity to give.

Indicators of wealth may include:

- Job title
- Home ownership
- Home value
- Business ownership
- Boat ownership
- Collections
- Other assets
- Other charitable giving

During your one-on-one interaction, you will ask questions of and actively listen to your prospect. As you are conversing with them, after you have connected on values and validated the potential donor's thoughts, feelings, and beliefs but before you make the ask, question them about what purpose they have in mind for the donation, the form the donation will take, the amount they are considering, the timing that is most comfortable for them, and the process they need to decide. Make sure you have all the information you need to structure a gift of the size you are asking.

Indicators of Business Capacity

The most obvious indicator of a business' capacity to give is the size of the business. Just because a business is big, though, doesn't mean it has the capacity to give. For-profit businesses, particularly small business, are often plagued by the same resource constraints a small to midsized nonprofit is. But sometimes they are not. A small business can be a high-profit venture just as much as they may be struggling to make ends meet.

Do your secondary research to see if you can assess profits. Large corporations often publish stockholder reports online. Some businesses are extremely active in supporting their communities and information about their charitable giving can be found on their websites. Sometimes businesses will even tell you what amounts they give out, the qualifications to be a recipient, and the process for accessing the money.

Just like with individual prospects, confirm whatever information you have gleaned from secondary research with primary research. Talk to a business professional and ask them questions. Dress in typical business attire when you visit them. Use their language, concepts, and words that are familiar to them and easy to understand. Match their style of presenting information, probably a direct, no nonsense, get-to-the-bottom-line type of approach. Be direct, forthright, honest, and straightforward. Be passionate about the potential partnership. Your genuineness will engender trust. Listen more than you talk; find out as much as you can about them. And unambiguously ask about their charitable giving.

Indicators of Foundation and Government Capacity

Foundation and government funders usually tell you how much they are willing to give. Either the amount will be in the application guidelines or, in the case of foundations, can be inferred from information gathered from their 990s. A foundation's 990 will tell you who their grant recipients were and how much the recipient received. Even if a funding range is given in the application guidelines, you want to go to the 990 to see exactly what they fund, where they fund, and how much they fund. Of course, if they allow it, you will want to confirm your findings one-on-one with a funding representative.

Overcoming Common Giving Concerns

Potential individual donors may shy away from agreeing to meetings where they will be asked for money. That is, if they don't know you or because you haven't established a relationship based on their goals and priorities. During my career, I haven't really run into many objections to meetings with me because I've done my homework.

Also in my experience, nonprofit leaders with the title development director or fundraiser are received with more skepticism than those with the title executive director or board member. That is because a development director's or fundraiser's job is perceived to be one of asking for money whereas an executive director's or board member's position is seen more broadly and not automatically associated with raising funds. That difference in perception is one reason why it's a good idea for a board member or executive director to work in tandem with their development director when pursuing large personal gifts.

Three of the most common objections are something along the lines of:

- "I already gave to XYZ organization."
- "I've had a bad experience with your nonprofit."
- "I've heard negative things about your agency."

How do you respond?

First and foremost, listen to what they have to say without getting defensive. You don't want to respond like you're being attacked. Because you and your nonprofit are not. The person on the other end is just expressing his or her hesitation to open their wallet yet again without any assurance that what they have to give will really make a difference or further their goals.

Acknowledge and validate their behaviors and beliefs. Validate doesn't necessarily mean you agree with them. It just means you listened and heard them. Engage in active listening. And then ask questions to understand the motivations behind their statements. Address the root issue.

Make the conversation about values and impact, not money. Congratulate the donor for their philanthropy elsewhere and encourage them to donate to your organization too. Don't get into the comparison game. That's a no-win situation where, even if you win, you lose. Just ask them if they would like to make an even bigger impact through additional giving.

If the person expresses negative perceptions about your agency, don't argue with them. Address your prospect's concerns and tell them what has been done to overcome the challenges. Reframe the conversation. Direct the discussion toward something that will turn the prospective donor's negative frame of mind around.

Working in Tandem with Your Development Director

You and your development director are a team with a powerful one-two punch, if you work together. As executive director, you can set up the environment for success. Your development director can then support you in your efforts.

Liaison to the Board

The first thing the development director will need from you is to encourage fundraising leadership from the board. As the chief volunteers of the agency, the board models how they want the community to interact with the organization. If board members do not give at a sacrificial level, community members have no leadership example to follow. If it is not important for the leaders of the nonprofit to give, then why should they?

The development director also needs board members to open doors for them. This doesn't mean board members hand over all their cell phone contacts for the staff to solicit. What it does mean is that board members actively participate in identifying friends, colleagues, and co-workers who can advance the work of the organization. And make any necessary introduction to the agency, helping to engage them in the nonprofit's mission. The development director is one person with limited contacts. He or she needs the help of the organization to develop more.

Meeting with Prospects

The development director will need you, the head of the agency, to meet with important prospects. As the executive director, you are your organization's liaison to the community, the public face of the agency. That is not a duty you want to shirk. Major donors, whether they be individuals, foundations, or businesses, want to meet with you to be assured that all is well at the agency.

And to make sure that whatever agreement is reached, you will do everything in your power to make sure its provisions are kept. You are the only staff person at the organization who can encumber the agency to ensure organizational performance. Your development director must know that you have their back as they make promises to the community.

Of course, the development director can support you by conducting research, managing logistics, coaching you, preparing documents, and maybe even accompanying you to meetings. If you have a development director, they are your partner when it comes to fundraising. You both need each other. Together, you both achieve more.

Frank's Solution

Frank had his development director conduct some research to see what other causes Linda and her husband supported. They found that Linda and her husband were very generous, giving to causes where the family had direct involvement.

Frank called Susan, his board president, to inquire whether she could accompany him to a breakfast or lunch meeting with Linda and her husband. Susan agreed.

Then Frank called Linda to see if she was interested in meeting to discuss the needs of adults with disabilities in their county. Linda was interested and they arranged a time and date for a breakfast meeting at a local restaurant. As they were ending the conversation, Frank mentioned that, in addition to information about the needs in the county, he would be bringing information about the impact his agency was having upon them.

Frank and Susan met Linda and her husband at the appointed time and place. Frank began the conversation by asking Linda about her cousin and how he was faring. Susan soon joined the discussion talking about her experiences as mother of a special needs child. Linda's attention peaked. The connection was made.

And soon the dialogue turned toward supporting the local disability community. Then Linda and her husband peppered Frank and Susan with questions about their nonprofit's impact in the local community.

The time came to ask Linda and her husband for financial support.

"Would you consider supporting our organization at a leadership level?" Frank asked.

"Yes," Linda replied.

"I was thinking something in the $100,000 range," Frank stated. "Is that comfortable for you?"

"We'll consider it," Linda's husband answered. "Let us get back to you once we see your financial position. I'd like to know more about your nonprofit and its sustainability. Once we review the materials, Linda will give you a call."

Frank smiled. "Thank you," he said.

Back in the office, Frank prepared a handwritten thank-you note, gathered the more in-depth flyers and brochures he had on hand, and put them in an envelope with the requested financials. He mailed them to the address Linda's husband had provided.

A few days later, he called Linda and asked her if they had received the materials he sent and if they had any questions.

"We don't have any questions," she replied, "But we don't feel comfortable making such a large one-time donation. Would $25,000 a year for four years still allow you to make the impact you described at our breakfast meeting?"

"Yes, for fewer people over a longer period of time," Frank told her. "Plus, the extended time factor will allow us to attract other leadership donors and leverage your contribution."

"I'd like to help you do that," Linda declared. "What are our next steps?"

"Thank you, thank you, thank you!" Frank responded. "Let me talk to my development director and I'll get back to you."

Wrapping It Up

Your first approach to potential donors is not an ask for money. The goal of your initial interaction is to connect, find information, and get a better understanding of each other. Ask them questions. Find out more about them. Give them an opportunity to feel understood and accepted. And talk about yourself too. Be authentic.

When you do ask them for money, don't ask them to complete two or more actions or give them choices. Be brief and get down to the point. Ask for a specific amount. And then don't say anything. Let them be the first to break the silence.

Thank your donors whenever they respond to a call to action, especially a call to donate. Let your donors know you appreciate their efforts on your nonprofit's behalf. Create a continuous cycle of donor engagement and mission fulfillment.

To discover a prospect's capacity to give, you need to conduct both secondary and primary research. The information gleaned from secondary research, however, should be confirmed through primary research. Primary research is the information gotten from people themselves through one-one interviews, focus groups, surveys, or observation.

If you do your homework, you're likely to run unto fewer obstacles when it comes to asking for donations. However, if you do run into roadblocks, first and foremost, listen to what is being said say without getting defensive. Acknowledge and validate their behaviors and beliefs. Address your prospect's concerns and tell them what has been done to overcome the challenges. Then direct the discussion toward something that will turn the prospective donor's negative frame of mind around.

You and your development director work together to make fundraising happen. You work with the board to lead the agency, prime the community, and support the promises made regarding fundraising agreements. Your development director supports you in conducting research, managing logistics, coaching you, preparing documents, and accompanying you to meetings. Together, you make an efficient and effective team.

Points to Remember

- Before you ask a prospect for money, build a strong relationship. Connect on values, listen more than you talk, and validate their perceptions and beliefs.

- When you make an ask for money, be clear, direct, and specific. Ask them to do only one thing—make a donation in the range of x amount.

- After a promise of a donation, acknowledge your donor's gift and validate their decision to give by thanking them, and thanking them often.

- To uncover a potential donor's capacity to give, conduct both secondary and primary research. Your primary research should take the form of a one-on-one interaction with your prospect where you can make observations and ask questions directly.

- If you encounter resistance to giving, listen to their objections, acknowledge what is being said, validate their perceptions, address their concerns, and reframe the conversation.

What's Next

Armed with the tools to make the ask, it's time to reach out to future donors. But where are they? Donors just don't just show up at your door. You need to go out and invite them in. And you need to be efficient in your efforts. **Chapter Ten** discusses how to get the most return on your investment when bringing future donors on board.

Chapter Ten

Becoming Well Known and Well Resourced

Tanya, the executive director of a regional job training agency, wanted to bring more business donors to her nonprofit. Her agency already enjoyed some corporate support, but the numbers of businesses who contributed had been more or less steady for more than five years. She knew there was more support out there. How could she attract the new donors she wanted?

Reaching Out to Your Community

Now that you know how to create fundraising efficiencies, prepare your nonprofit for fundraising success, fund your growth, set up set up evaluation metrics, tame your fundraising fears, and make the ask, your challenge is to go out into the community and find people to support your cause who have the capability to give. And do it with limited resources. The most important principle to remember when you reach out to your community is to spend your time and money where it will bear the most fruit, where you can get the biggest bang for your buck.

As I explained in *The Sustainable High ROI Fundraising System*, you start by identifying, researching, and then speaking to the specific groups you want to reach. Research and learn about your potential donors. Get evidence of what they think and use that information to create effective communication campaigns. Allocate resources to reach people with a propensity toward your cause, not just anybody. You want to get the most out of your scarce resources.

Respond to your community and people will respond to you. Come from their viewpoint, incorporating the words and concepts that excite them into your outreach. Each population segment will have its own set of priorities, interests, and preferences. For best results, messages to each group need to be personalized. And each group will be found someplace different than the other groups. That's one reason why you want to target specific groups: it takes resources to effectively reach different population segments. And you want to expend your resources where they will produce the most lucrative results.

Stick to your mission in all you do, including your fundraising. You want to be known for the mission your nonprofit meets instead of the money you need. It is mission that motivates donors to give. Foundations give to nonprofits who meet their missions. Businesses give to nonprofits that have a strong sense of corporate identity, in other words, a strong mission orientation. And individuals want to make an impact in the community; an impact that is defined by your mission.

Create and maintain consistent, strong messaging through good branding, articulating a unique marketing position, making your message a mainstay of your culture, and spreading your message extensively. Make sure your message is unified so there is no confusion about who your nonprofit is and what it stands for.

So, who do you focus your efforts on? How do you identify the target groups you want to reach? And what questions do you ask them once you reach them?

Recognize Your Key Stakeholders

Your key stakeholders include your board, staff, clients, volunteers, donors, collaborators, and community leaders. There may be others, depending on your goals. To get a complete view of what the whole community knows and thinks about your agency, you want to gather input from all your important constituencies. And then, as we said above, use their feedback to develop targeted campaigns directed to them.

Start with those closest to your organization: your board and staff. Elicit their thoughts and opinions about your organization. (I give suggested questions in the next section.) Your board and staff know your agency most intimately and can most easily carry your nonprofit's banner into the community.

That means your board needs to be engaged with your agency. And that encompasses talking to them about strategy and outcomes as opposed to operations. You do not want your board to be consumed with the nitty-gritty details of running your nonprofit. You need to make their experiences meaningful. You want them to be happy mission ambassadors for you. We talked about engaging your board in fundraising in **Chapter Three**.

Make sure your staff are satisfied with their experiences at your organization as well. If agency morale is low, you will have a hard time overcoming your reputation. I once worked for a nonprofit that had a great mission but high staff dissatisfaction. The staff loved working with the clients but felt the work environment was oppressive. And it showed in their turnover rates. Every piece of good PR that agency got was counterbalanced with a negative buzz among former employees. So, it behooves your fundraising to keep staff morale up.

> **Shifting Mindset**
>
> Staff morale has a lot to do with fundraising.

Move on to your donors. Gather input from not only your individual donors, but also foundation and business donor representatives. Elicit their opinions and thoughts about your nonprofit. Get their feedback.

Don't forget about your volunteers and advocates. They can provide an important perspective too.

You also want the perspective of the people you serve.

You can get a rough idea of how you are perceived in the business community be getting feedback from your vendors. Vendors are an often-overlooked source of support, through either donations or discounts. Vendors are vested in your success. They want you to grow and purchase more of their goods or services.

Who are your collaborators? Get their feedback too.

Who are your community leaders—the business, civic, and religious leaders? You want their opinions as well.

And, finally, who are your competitors? They are an often-overlooked source of information. What do they think of your organization?

Key Stakeholder Interviews

Ask all these groups for feedback and advice. People love giving their opinions. And use the questions here:

1. Tell me a little about what you know of [nonprofit].

2. When you think of [nonprofit], what is the first thing you think of?

3. What do you think the most important thing [nonprofit] does is?

4. What appeals most to you about [nonprofit]?

5. How did you first hear about [nonprofit]?

6. Tell me a little about your involvement with [nonprofit].

7. Would you or are you considering increasing your support through volunteering or donating to [nonprofit]?

8. Why or why not?

9. What would move you to be more engaged with [nonprofit]?

10. What one piece of advice would you give to [nonprofit] so that it is better able to advance its mission?

Be short, sweet, and to the point. Don't take a lot of time and do not ask them for money. What you are doing is laying the foundation for future interactions, seeing what different stakeholder groups think about your agency and the importance of what your organization does. Your goal is the same one that we talked about in **Chapter Nine**—to connect, find information, and get a better understanding of one another.

Identifying Potential Donors

Donations come from individuals, foundations, businesses, and government contracts. But not all donors and opportunities should be pursued. Pursue only those prospects who are interested in your mission or where the purpose of the funding advances your agency's mission. The process for identifying individuals and business donors is different than the one to identify foundation and government donors.

Identifying Individual and Business Prospects

As we discussed in **Chapter Three,** calculating donors' lifetime values and targeting donor groups similar to the those with the highest amounts is one tactic to identify new supporters. Another is to start with your innermost circle, the bullseye as I call it in *The Sustainable High ROI Fundraising System*, and move out from there. In other words, reach out to the contacts of your board, staff, volunteers, and current donors. And then, once you have a relationship with them, contact their contacts. Your objective is to have as many people as possible connecting with others and becoming mission ambassadors for your organization.

Think of all connections people can have to other people. Have your development committee brainstorm all their connections including:

- Family members
- Friends
- Co-workers
- Fellow college alumni
- Fellow high school alumni
- Fellow civic group members
- Fellow house of worship attenders
- Fellow sports team members
- Parents of child's friends
- Service providers
- Social contacts

Then think of all the other connections your organization has. For example:

- Supporters of organizations with similar missions
- Businesses with shared client target groups
- Manufacturers of products that your nonprofit or your clients use
- Service providers related to your mission and programs

Write down everything you know about that person or entity. For example, their target market; political, social, or religious affiliations; family or business situations; hobbies; interests; community involvement; state of health; personality or brand traits; familiarity with your organization; and degree of involvement with your organization. You may think of others.

Not that you will approach all these people or businesses. In addition to a connection, potential donors also need an affinity for your cause and the ability to give. You need to screen for that and you screen through secondary and primary research. We talked about conducting secondary and primary research in **Chapter Five**.

Identifying Foundation Prospects

Foundations are required by law to file a 990 every year. The 990 contains the foundation's mission, its board members, its funding guidelines, and its funding recipients. Perusing 990s helps you discern exactly what type of organizations are funded and what the foundation's range of funding is. Use that information to ascertain whether your program is a good fit or not.

You can find 990s in a number of places. Foundation Directory Online, Foundation Search, and Instrumentl are three databases that are easy to search—there are many others—and are accessed via paid subscriptions. You can also find 990s on GuideStar, which is free.

If it appears that your program matches the purpose of their funding, you continue your research. Go to the foundation prospects' websites, if they have one. Websites are helpful for gleaning information about funders in their own words. Besides that, you usually gain more information.

You can confirm information gleaned from the 990s, get a history of the foundation and an understanding of why it exists, see their press releases, annual reports, and position or research papers through information on their website. These documents can play a crucial role in understanding what the funder's strategies are or what their preferred solutions to stated problems are. Most importantly, the website will give you up-to-date application forms and guidelines.

You want to thoroughly do your research before making personal contact so that you can show foundation officers that you will not waste their time. Grant writing doesn't start with the first call or letter. The relationship begins with the research.

Identifying Governmental Prospects

Government funders are easy to identify in the sense that there is usually plenty of public information available about them. The information, however, is not always easy to find and can be very time consuming to look for. You might have a lot of information to dig through.

For federal grants, usually grant competitions are announced through a notice of funding availability, or NOFA. You can find NOFAs in the Federal Register, which you can receive daily through a listserv, through the grants.gov website, or through an individual federal agency's website. Most states have similar mechanisms customized to the laws of that state.

> **Clarifying Point**
>
> There is usually a lot of public information about government funding opportunities but it can be onerous to find.

Sometimes NOFAs come in parts and with some period of time between the parts. Both NOFA sections will apply to your application. Your budget and contract guidelines might be found in separate Office of Management and Budget Circulars. You should be familiar with all applicable regulations and publications before you start writing your applications to make sure your programs' methodology and budget address all the required guidelines.

Sometimes governmental funding is announced through requests for proposals, or RFPs. State, county, and municipal funding is usually less onerous to apply for than federal funding. However, a large percentage of state and local governmental funding is passed through to them from the federal government. In those cases, federal requirements apply to even local government allocations.

The allocation of government funding is dictated by legislation. Get a copy of these laws and study them. Understand the purpose of the legislation. Understand who makes the funding decisions and what the process will be. Know all the rules and how they are interpreted *before* you put 100 or more hours in writing an application that doesn't meet all the funding requirements.

As we mentioned in **Chapter Six**, the funding provided to fulfill administrative and reporting requirements is often less than actual costs. Make sure you can cover those extra costs if you get the funding. If you can't, then the opportunity is not a good fit or potential funding source.

Indicators of Propensity to Give

Just because a person or entity has a formal or informal connection to you, or your agency, doesn't mean that they will give. They also need to have an affinity for your cause and the capacity to give. You do not want to focus on donors who have no interest in giving to you. You want to focus your time and efforts where they are likely to bear fruit. So, you need to pay attention to indicators of a prospect's propensity to give.

Interest

Whether they are potential individual, business, or foundation donors, all of them are represented by people. Governmental entities are staffed by people too, so some of the concepts discussed in the section about gauging interest from people will apply. When dealing with government representatives, though, there are additional concerns that I have outlined in a separate section.

Gauging Interest from People

One indicator of interest people have in your cause is how warmly or coolly the first contact is received. People who are interested in what you have to say will generally greet you more warmly than those who don't. The level of the warmth of the reception should be noted in the donor record.

A cool reception does not necessarily mean there is no interest, though. The prospect may be having a bad day or struggling with an emergent financial situation or distracted for some other reason. The timing may not be right. They may also be wary of your motivations, as we talked about in **Chapter Nine**. If that's the case, you

> ### Food for Thought
>
> A cool reception does not necessarily indicate a lack of interest.

need to take more time to establish trust. So, if you do receive a cool reception, note it and, unless you get a firm 'no', follow up at a later time.

Another indicator of interest is the length of the conversation. Longer conversations usually indicate a higher level of connection and engagement. The length of your conversation should also be noted in the donor record.

If someone is really engaged and level of trust has been established, the prospect will start revealing personal details. Write these details down. For example, political affiliation, religious affiliation, employment details, family facts, interests, hobbies, community involvement, state of heath, personality traits, and so on.

If the person is revealing facts about themselves, then the time has come to confirm the findings of your secondary research. You can also start asking the questions we outlined in the previous section. Make sure, too, that you record answers in the donor record.

After the conversation is over, rate the quality of conversation with the potential donor. Also rate the interest expressed in your cause as well as your specific organization. Note the explicit issue the donor wants to help solve and how important it is to them that it be solved. Try to quantify their answers in dollars and cents. Again, record your valuations in the donor record.

Make sure to follow up with any promises you made or requests for more information they asked for. For example, will you send them literature? Or follow up with an email? Or a phone call? Or an in-person visit? Or something else?

Gauging Interest from Government Representatives

The motivations of legislators are very different than those of individuals, foundations or businesses. As we discussed in **Chapter Six**, legislators are motivated by voter concerns. They will answer questions from the public, as the public is who they are serving and who keeps them in office.

The trick is to really get their attention. Do you know what issues are important to your community? Have you asked them? Do you sit on community boards? Do you know what issues are coming up for a vote? What are the voter's concerns? How do you know? Find out the answers and use them as the basis for talking to a legislator. Then use the length of conversation, the body language, and the questions elected officials ask as indicators of their interest.

Means

During the conversation, in addition to their level of interest, you will also be assessing their means to give. We talked about uncovering their capacity to give in **Chapter Nine**.

Take the information you glean and quantify an amount for the ask. If you have developed enough trust in your relationship, you can even ask the potential donor how much it is worth to them in dollars and cents to help solve the issue they care about. Now, you have a reliable amount on which to base your ask.

Next, you need to assess when the right time is to ask for the donation. And you will need to start making arrangements about who and where to make the ask.

Attracting and Engaging Potential Donors

Step four of The Sustainable High ROI Fundraising System involves exciting your community so that they eagerly support your agency. In the book *The Sustainable High ROI Fundraising System,* we talk at length about what it takes to gain visibility in the community, engage people in your cause, and attract the donor support you desire. We go back to those concepts here, applying those strategies to specific donor groups—individual, foundation, business, and government—and expanding the discussion we began in **Chapter Six** about approaching different types of donors.

Get Your Messaging Right

The purpose of identifying and getting feedback from your key stakeholders is to develop messages that can be used to increase your base of support. The most effective messages are the ones potential donors will relate to. As we explained earlier in the chapter, you use their input to ascertain the words and concepts that excite others, the information channels they prefer, and the work you have to do to get the word out about your organization.

When you formulate your messages, make them about them. Talk to them about meeting their needs and goals instead of how great your nonprofit is. While you will attract some support for your organization spouting off its accomplishments, it is not your agency that excites people. What excites people is the opportunities they have to make the impact they desire. In other words, how they can participate in fulfilling the mission.

> **Words of Wisdom**
>
> When you formulate your messages, talk to potential donors about meeting their needs and goals instead of how great your nonprofit is.

To get people involved, directly ask them. Every public message you deliver—be it a press release, social media post, advertisement, or speech, to name a few—should have a call to action with a clear way to get involved in your organization's work. Whether you ask them to like and follow you on social media to help you spread the word, advocate for policy change that will improve the world they live in, vote so their voice is heard, come to an event to meet like-minded people, or donate to further the cause they believe in – whatever it is – it is important that you ask. If you don't ask, you don't get. Always have a clear call to action.

And in your call to action, tell them the benefit that results from completing whatever you're asking them to do. It's important to outline the benefits of completing what you've asked them. Let them know how they will fulfill their values and reach their goals by performing that task. Use the information you found when surveying your key stakeholders to understand their motivations. And, to emphasize, make the call to action and its benefits about them, not your nonprofit or its needs.

Collecting Individual Donor Leads

Target specific potential donor groups with the messages you've created. As we talked about in **Chapter Five**, a good way to segment groups is by the values they hold and the communication channels they prefer. One method of identifying these values, is by studying your highest donor's lifetime values and base your profile on them.

You target specific groups rather than everyone so that you ensure your message resonates with those most likely to give and resources are used where they produce the highest results. Casting a small net where you find more people likely to give yields better returns than casting a large net where you find a lot of people but don't know their propensity to give.

Your aim is to talk to and develop a relationship with the potential donors belonging to the groups you have identified. In addition to the relationship-based donor acquisition techniques we've been describing so far, you can generate individual leads through your website, social media efforts, and cultivation events.

Website

Your website should target specific groups, just like any other communication channel. And one of those groups is your potential donors. If you have done your homework, you know exactly who you are trying to reach. In turn, then, you know who to target your messages toward.

You use those same basic messages in your direct mail and social media acquisition campaigns. Design specific campaigns for this effort.

And use them to obtain email addresses and drive traffic to your website so that you can grow your email list. Once people's names are on your email list, you can build deeper relationships with them and send them even more targeted information, culminating in a call to action. Once a solid relationship is built, your call to action can be a request for a donation.

Once people get to your website, you want them to leave their names. The theory is that if a person is interested in your website, there is probably an interest in your cause. Encourage them to leave their name by offering something on your website for free in exchange for their email. You can use your key stakeholder feedback to inform your choice of freebie.

Social Media

For your social media campaigns to be effective, posts must be regular, frequent, and interesting. You need to be frequent to be remembered. You need to be interesting to capture people's attention. Short videos and pictures with captions capture the most attention.

Use different types of social media posts to create awareness and engage prospects. For example:

- Tag people involved with your nonprofit.
- Post short success stories around your nonprofit's mission.
- Spotlight your volunteers, donors, and board members.
- Use infographics to make a point.
- Conduct surveys.
- Use your grant needs assessments to create myth buster posts
- Help people get to know your organization by sharing an historical fact or milestone.
- Make pre-event announcements and post event thank-you messages and results.
- If you have built a relationship, make an appeal for donations.

The list is endless. Be creative. Just be brief, concise, and generate interest. Make the content interactive. Respond to people who comment. Track what posts give you the most likes and comments and do more posts like them. You are part of a huge community conversation, building a relationship with an online community rather than an individual. We talked about relationship building in **Chapter Nine**.

Cultivation Events

You can also engage potential donors through cultivation events, such as house parties, coffee get-togethers, or other private group meetings. To run a successful cultivation event:

1. Target who you want to reach.

2. Design the type of event you want to hold. Use your stakeholder feedback to brainstorm your choices.

3. Find a host for the event. This should not be you, the executive director. It should be a peer of the people you want to invite.

4. Find a time that works for your host and is convenient for your target group.

5. Find a location. Again, let your stakeholder feedback inform your choices.

6. Send the invitation—under the name of the host, not you, the executive director.

7. Plan the agenda. Make it mission related and do not include an ask. Your goal, just as with individuals, is to connect and get a better understanding of one another.

8. Hold the event.

9. Follow up with attendees.

The follow up is important because that is when you can really start building strong one-on-one relationships and engage the potential donor even more with your nonprofit. For more information about cultivation events, see *The Nonprofit Quick Guide: How to Run a Successful Cultivation Event.*

Getting the Attention of Businesses

To get the attention of the business community, you need to do two things: create awareness of and differentiate your nonprofit from all other nonprofits. Cultivation events are good vehicles for engaging them with your organization.

Creating Awareness in the Business Community

You create awareness of your nonprofit by being visible. Involvement with your local, regional, and state Chambers of Commerce, Business and Industry chapter, Rotary Club, and other business groups are a good place to start. At the very least, you want to attend their networking events. If they have an annual dinner, you want to be there too. If they have regular meetings, you may want to consider attending so that other group members get to know and remember you.

If you want to make even more of impression, you can join a committee or workgroup. Active committee participation demonstrates what you, and by association your nonprofit, can bring to the table. Serving on a committee also gives you a chance to gain exposure for your organization and cause business leaders to think of you as a peer.

In addition to networking and participating in workgroups, radio spots, TV stories, and print articles create visibility for your agency, including within the business community. Explore advertising in business publications, guesting on business-focused radio and TV programs, contributing articles to business-directed magazines, newspapers, and other publications, or sponsoring a business event.

You can also draw the attention of the business community by designing your website so that it contains keywords that business professionals may use in an internet search. Cultivation events are also a good way to introduce your nonprofit to business professionals.

To target specific businesses, like and follow them on social media. Forward and share their posts that are of interest to your donors, volunteers, advocates, and community partners. Tag specific businesses as part of your social media strategy. And mention them in posts you write.

Differentiating Your Nonprofit

You create differentiation by developing a unique marketing position statement. A unique marketing position is what your agency brings to the community that no other nonprofit like you brings. It tells the world where your organization fits into the landscape of all the other nonprofits, what your agency's niche is, and what makes your organization different. Once you know how your nonprofit is different than any other, you can start building clear, unifying messages around that uniqueness.

After you have differentiated your nonprofit and gotten noticed, if you really want to stand out, don't approach businesses asking for money. It's not how to start relationships. Instead, ask how you can help them meet their business goals.

Be a partner with them. With businesses, it is an exchange relationship where both parties give and receive something of value. If you approach them asking to enter into a relationship that meets their goals, you will get much farther along than if you come across as a beggar asking for a handout. And you are more likely to be successful in getting a donation.

Cultivation Events

You can hold cultivation events with business prospects just as with individual prospects. The principles are the same. All that is changing is your target audience. Which, in turn, affects the type of event you plan, who your host is, and possibly the time and place of the event.

Foundations

After you have done your research, if the foundation welcomes inquiries, call, e-mail or write to them to ask for any updated guidelines, interests, or other information. Calling or writing for information is often the first impression a foundation has of you and your organization. When you do make contact, you want them to know you have their interests in mind and can follow any directions they have provided. In short, you want to show them that you can be an excellent conduit for their funds.

When writing grant requests, watch for errors in name, address, salutation, spelling, grammar and math. Make sure everything mentioned in the narrative is reflected in the budget and every line item in the budget is described in the narrative.

Always be courteous and respectful. It is also important to be authentic, honest, and forthright. In addition, it will help if you acknowledge and validate the person you speak to, as we discussed in **Chapter Nine**. It's people who answer the phone, read the proposal, make the decisions, and report back to their board and the IRS.

Government Officials

Approach elected officials about potential funding opportunities that have not yet been legislated or allocated. You, as a 501(c)(3), may not be able to lobby for specific legislation, but you can advocate for your cause and educate your legislators about community issues.

Do you know what issues are important to your community? Have you asked them? Do you sit on community boards? Do you survey your clients, staff, volunteers, or donors? What are their concerns? How do you know?

> **Food for Thought**
>
> You, as a non profit, *can* advocate for your cause and educate your legislators about community issues and educate your community about legislative issues.

You can also educate the community about legislative issues. Which means you may be able to arrange for legislators to speak to constituencies of yours that vote. Which means visibility for the elected officials. Do you offer any fundraising or networking events where they can speak to potential voters? What about your communication channels with clients, staff, volunteers, donors, and partner agencies—can you leverage them?

After funds have become available is when you talk to government employees. They will always help you as part of their job is to give everyone equal opportunity. Although they will not be able to influence the decision-making process, they can guide you through the rules and regulations governing that process and help you navigate the complexities of an application.

Retaining Donors

Donor retention comes from good stewardship of existing and newly acquired donors and telling them the results their donation made. And then re-cultivating them.

Stewardship

New donors should be immediately thanked and engaged. To do this, set up a series of welcome emails to send to new donors.

1. The first email is an immediate acknowledgement of the gift. This should be generated by your online gift processing software.

2. The second email, sent within 24 hours of making the gift, is an individualized email thanking the donor for the gift and telling them the impact their gift made on meeting community needs.

3. The third email, sent about two weeks after the gift is made, is a donor welcome packet.

4. The fourth email is asking for feedback.

Donors cannot be thanked enough. You want to thank them often and through a number of channels. For example, you can recognize donors:

- on your website
- in your newsletters
- on your signage
- in your annual reports
- through donor appreciation events

No one I know has ever been offended by being thanked too much. Your donors are heroes in making the mission possible. Let them know it. Thank them promptly and often.

Reporting

Not only do you need to thank your donors, you also need to tell them how their donations were used. Not in terms of meeting agency needs, but in terms of the impact they have made in solving the issue they were interested in alleviating.

For example, don't just tell them how people many you fed, also tell them the impact that providing nutritious food had on the people you fed. Feeding people not only fills their stomachs, but also prevents chronic disease and theft. And preventing chronic disease and theft reduces the community's costs for healthcare and policing. If you're feeding children, providing meals improves learning which increases graduation rates which leads to a more prepared workforce and less dependence on government programs, decreasing societal costs.

And make it personal. Tell a story about how someone's life was changed.

So, when you report on results, think through the impact. It may be more significant than it appears.

Re-cultivation

Your job does not stop with thanking donors. Once a donor is thanked, if you want another donation, you immediately start re-cultivating them. The key is to keep them engaged. Donors who are engaged are much more likely to repeat and even increase their donations. Get to know your donors. Make your interactions a two-way relationship.

Ask for feedback about their experiences. Get them talking. Continue to build relationships. Ask your donors to do something, like respond to a poll, share a social media post, attend a community event, sign a petition, ask a neighbor to join them at an event, or something else. Take the relationship to the next level.

Then ask them how else they would like to be involved with your organization. They may wish to volunteer. They may want to meet a board member. They may want a leadership experience. They may want to hobnob with other donors. They may want to learn new skills. They may want an exclusive social experience. The list goes on. Structure experiences that are meaningful for them.

Don't always ask for money. Donors often complain that the only time they hear from a nonprofit is when it needs money. Let them know how important a relationship with them is to you, beyond money. Let them know you know they are more than ATMs and appreciate them as whole people. In word and deed.

Reaching Mission and Financial Sustainability

You not only need to increase revenues, you also need to build wealth. It's not only net income that counts. You need to focus on building your assets too.

The goal of increasing your fundraising efficiencies is to advance your agency's mission, meeting more community need and affecting social change. Which means achieving financial and mission sustainability. You need money to grow your programs and advance your mission. And it is fulfillment of mission that motivates donors to give. You need both mission and money to move your organization forward. Sustainability must be achieved on both fronts. The two are inextricably linked.

The first step to reach sustainability is to realize continual increases in revenues. Which means steadily acquiring new donors and moving existing donors up the donation ladder. Which means constantly identifying, recruiting, and retaining donors and asking them for sacrificial donations. There are only two ways to increase fundraising revenues: increase the number of donations and increase the amount of donations. We talked about identifying, recruiting, and retaining donors earlier in the chapter. We talked about asking them for money in **Chapter Nine**. For a complete discussion on how to motivate people to support your nonprofit, see my book *The Sustainable High ROI Fundraising System*.

The second step to achieve sustainability is to manage costs such that you realize continuous net surpluses. The best way to realize positive net income is by ensuring costs are less than revenues. We talked about budgeting for growth in **Chapter Three**.

As you grow, you need more staff. We explore how to build your team and afford their talent in **Chapter Eleven**. We go into greater detail regarding managing growth cycles in **Chapter Sixteen**.

But you can't just increase net income. You also need to build wealth. You need to grow the balance sheet just as much as the profit and loss statement. Refer back to **Chapter Four** for more information about wealth building.

Tanya's Solution

Tanya's first step was to brainstorm all her agency business connections, do some internet research on them, and then call them. Once she reached the proper contact, she recorded the information she was able to glean about the company and how well her call was received.

But contacting individual connections took a lot of time. Time she didn't have. So, she asked her development director to plan a business networking event where she could talk to them as a group. She suggested her development director interview a handful of businesses to ascertain how they perceived the nonprofit and what their greatest business needs were.

Based on the business' feedback, she and the development director created outreach materials for them. The final packet included a business case for support, a one-page overview of the financial and business position of the job training agency, and opportunities for their involvement.

Tanya decided to hold two networking events annually. She and her development director planned an agenda to include testimonials from a client the organization was currently serving and a business partner who donated to the agency and was willing to share why. They also presented a call to action for one-on-one meetings.

The first meeting had a lower than desired attendance. The second was better. The third was even more full. Soon Tanya had more requests for meetings than she had time for.

Wrapping It Up

The most important principle to remember when you reach out to your community is to spend your time and money where you have the greatest chance of realizing a high return on your investment. Reach out to your community coming from the perspective of your potential donor, incorporating the words and concepts that excite them into your outreach. You get those words and concepts from key stakeholder feedback.

Identify potential individual and business donors by mining your organization's connections, foundation donors by researching their 990s, and government donors by combing through NOFAs. Indicators of a prospect's propensity to give includes how warmly or coolly the first contact is received, the length of the conversation. Longer conversations usually indicate a higher level of connection and engagement, and whether the person reveals personal details.

Generate individual leads by offering an incentive for your website visitors to leave their name and email address. Follow up with targeted email campaigns to them. To reach the business community, create awareness and differentiate your nonprofit from all other nonprofits. Use cultivation events to encourage interaction with your agency and share how you help the community. Talk to legislators about voter concerns,

Set up a series of welcome emails to send to new donors to thank them, engage them, and improve their retention. Tell them how their donations were used in terms of the impact they have made, not on the organization, but on the alleviation of community need. If you want another donation, keep them engaged. Make your interactions a two-way relationship.

To reach financial and mission sustainability, continually increase your revenues, contain costs, manage growth, and build wealth. Pay attention to the balance sheet just as much as the profit and loss statement.

Points to Remember

- Identify and cultivate the specific donor groups you want to reach, those with the propensity and capability. Identify the potential donors who have the greatest capacity by calculating donor lifetime values and targeting community members who have a profile similar to your most valuable donors.

- Use key stakeholder feedback to inform messaging when reaching out to your community. Use the words and concepts that excite your key stakeholders to inform your messaging.

- You can generate giving leads by identifying your agency's connections, capturing names and emails on your website, and holding cultivation events. Qualify your leads by gauging interest in your cause and capability to give. Retain the donors you've worked so hard to get by immediately thanking them, sending them welcome messages, and letting them know the full impact of their donation.

What's Next

So, you're growing your organization and moving toward sustainability. Now you need people to execute the fundraising initiatives to get there. The next chapter addresses the makeup of your dream development team and how to afford talent within the confines of a limited budget.

Chapter Eleven

The Dream Team

C arlos was finally at the stage where he could afford to hire a development director. Although fundraising results were adequate, the elder care support agency needed to step up its game if it wanted to keep up with demand for services. The board realized that if the nonprofit was going to grow, it needed to add staff.

The organization had just received an unexpected large gift and decided to set aside a portion of it toward building a development department. Carlos now wanted to know what kind of staff to hire for the best return on the agency's salary investment. And when he could expect to see the results of the organization's investment.

The Effective Fundraising Team

Fundraising is a team sport. To effectively implement The Sustainable High ROI Fundraising System, you need board, staff, and volunteers all working together to achieve two objectives: promote mission and raise money. Your goal is to have as many people as possible advocating for your agency in the community, attracting the support you desire. And who better to do that than those closest to your organization?

This chapter outlines how to structure your fundraising dream team of board members, development professionals, and fundraising volunteers so that you leverage human resources as much as possible.

Board Member Leadership

Board members may not think fundraising is part of their core responsibilities, but it is. For example, a board approves a strategic plan, of which fundraising is part. The board approves a gift acceptance policy. The board approves the annual budget, which includes fundraising revenue goals and cost allocations. As civic leaders, the board primes the community for staff to be successful. As organizational leaders, the board also teaches the community how to interact with the nonprofit they serve regarding its programs, services, advocacy, and fundraising.

It is important that board members take the lead in fundraising. This doesn't necessarily mean they ask for money, and it definitely doesn't mean they plan events or wordsmith the annual appeal letter. No. Board members should not be involved in directing any day-to-day operations of the agency, including fundraising. Rather, you need board leadership that promotes your nonprofit to the community, getting them excited about your mission, and promoting your nonprofit's ability to make an impact. You also need your board to model the fundraising culture they create. Usually this is accomplished through the work of a development committee.

Governance and Fundraising

The board's role in fundraising is strategic rather than operational. Governance is setting policy for and determining the organization's strategic direction and assuring its design, creation, and accountability. The board's job in fundraising is to strategically allocate resources and monitor their acquisition. To do their job effectively, they need to be asking questions like the ones I postulated in my companion book *The Sustainable High ROI Fundraising System*:

- Are we fulfilling our duties to provide resources to implement and grow our mission?

- What strategies are we going to allocate resources toward to meet our mission?

- Do we have a written strategic plan that we regularly review and update?

- Are we constantly promoting mission in all we do, even in our fundraising strategy?

- Have we provided a favorable environment for the executive director and staff to succeed in raising money? For example, do we have written board giving and gift acceptance policies in place that we enforce?

- Where will we realize the most financial and mission return on our investment in fundraising?

- How do we want the community to interact with us? How do we as a board influence them to respond the way we want them to?

- Are we making progress in meeting our mission and financial goals?

Notice that these are strategic, not operational, questions. The board's job is not to run the agency. Rather, the board's job is to provide an environment that supports the executive director and staff in executing the strategies they have deemed most effective. It is the executive director's and staff's jobs to abide by the policies the board has set and implement the activities that fulfill the strategic objectives that meet the board's goals.

The Development Committee

Every board should have a development committee consisting of board members, staff, and fundraising volunteers. The committee serves as the bridge between the governance activities of the board and the operational activities of the staff. Its purpose is to lead board member participation in fundraising. A development committee brings together board members, staff, and volunteers to work cohesively together to meet the fundraising objectives of the agency.

Development committee responsibilities include proposing fundraising policies and procedures, developing the agency funding plan, overseeing fundraising activities, monitoring performance, evaluating results against the plan, and ensuring board involvement in fundraising.

The development committee is the board's central source of fundraising information. It helps board members understand what resources are needed to realize its goals and fulfill the nonprofit's mission.

The chair of the committee should be a board member. The responsibilities of the chair are to provide leadership to the committee and advocate for the initiatives it agrees on to the whole board.

A development committee description may look like the following:

Sample Development Committee Position Description

- Work with appropriate staff to develop a long-range and short-range development plan.

- Plan and oversee all fundraising efforts of the organization and appoint committee members to oversee fundraising activities.

- Assure full board participation in all campaigns and projects.

- Be familiar with the theory and techniques of development programs.

- Advocate to the full board the importance of fundraising in meeting the nonprofit's mission.

- Encourage the participation of all board members in fundraising activities and programs.

- Attend the agency's fundraising activities.

- Develop a plan to increase community involvement with the organization.

Structuring Your Staff

Board members are only one part of your dream team. Your development staff make up make up a second part—the part that you have to pay. As such, it is important that you organize your development department to ensure the donor experience is smooth and asking people for money is seamless.

In my companion book *The Sustainable High ROI Fundraising System*, we summarize typical fundraising staff roles—development director, grant writer, special events coordinator, major gifts officer, planned giving officer, director of foundations, and director of corporate relations. Most small to mid-sized nonprofits, out of necessity, hire generalists who can do a little bit of everything to be their development directors. But then they build toward staff specialization, not realizing that as they do, the focus of their fundraising program moves from centering around donor relationships to implementing the processes involved in gift giving.

As your organization grows, instead of hiring traditional fundraising specialists, I recommend hiring more fundraising generalists. Build a team with similar skills and complementary strengths around your donors' needs, not your fundraising methods. In his book ***Personalized Philanthropy: Crash the Fundraising Matrix***, Steven Meyers calls these fundraisers enlightened generalists. Enlightened generalists are fundraisers who are trained and experienced in all avenues donors use to bestow gifts. They do not specialize in any one method.

The Optimal Management Matrix

If you hire more enlightened generalists to staff your development department, the management matrix will look something like this:

Fundraising Generalist Management Matrix

	Researching	Cultivating	Asking	Stewarding
Development Director	Individual Donor Group 1	→		
Donor Relations Manager 1	Individual Donor Group 2	→		
Donor Relations Manager 2	Individual Donor Group 3	→		
Donor Relations Manager 3	Individual Donor Group 3	→		
Grant Writer	Foundation and Government Funders	→		

A traditional fundraising matrix looks something like this:

Traditional Development Offices

	Grant Writing	Annual Appeal	Special Events	Major Giving	Planned Giving	Corporate Giving
Donor 1						
Donor 2						
Donor 3						
Donor 4						
Donor 5						
Donor 6						
Donor 7						

The differences between the two are subtle but striking.

Differences Between Traditional Development Offices and the New Paradigm

Traditional Development Office	New Paradigm
Employs all fundraising methods	Employs all fundraising methods
Fundraiser involved with one fundraising method	Fundraiser involved with multiple fundraising methods
Donor involved with multiple fundraising staff	Donor involved with one fundraiser
Requires hiring multiple specialized fundraising staff	Requires hiring fundraising enlightened generalists
Emphasizes implementing correct fundraising methods and processes	Emphasizes building donor relationships

Your Ideal Development Department

A fully staffed development department will look something like this:

Dream Development Department

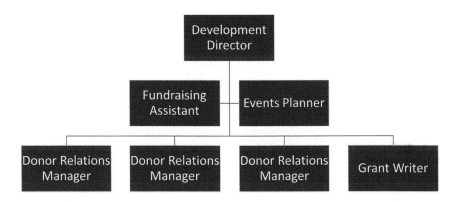

For a more comprehensive discussion on building your development team, see my companion book *The Sustainable High ROI Fundraising System*.

Affording Talent on a Shoestring Budget

So, how do you afford to hire development staff who are skilled, qualified, and experienced, especially if you are a small to midsized nonprofit? Don't these types of candidates apply to the jobs that pay well, usually found in big organizations?

The answer is no. You can have highly skilled staff at your organization. And I'll tell you how.

Hire an experienced development director as your second or third hire. You need someone in your organization who can bring in resources you can use for growth. You don't have to hire full time. I have had good luck hiring older workers who no longer wished to work full time.

And I didn't pay them an astronomical amount. I was fair, to be sure. Development directors deserve to be paid fairly. But I wasn't paying at the high end of the scale either. What these development directors found exciting about the opportunity I offered was I wanted the nonprofit to grow, and I gave my staff the freedom to chart a course to get me there within their field of expertise. That's an exciting proposition for a development professional. Shaping the future of an agency is not something that happens every day. It is very motivating.

Maybe you should look at the kind of leadership opportunities you are providing to attract an affordable, experienced professional. You may also need to improve the wording you use so that it adequately reflects all that you're offering. We explore recruiting good fundraising staff in **Chapter Twelve**.

> ### Encouragement
>
> You can find good development professionals to work for you if you offer shared leadership opportunities and other non-monetary perks.

You may also need to kill your scarcity mindset. If you think you can't get good help, you probably won't. As we talked about in **Chapter Four**, your mindset has a lot to do with your success. Finding the perfect candidate may take more time than you want, but there are potential employees out there. We describe what attracts good fundraising team members to an agency in **Chapter Twelve**.

Plan for staff growth. Don't just wait for it to happen—engineer it. And plot out how you're going to fund it. Talk strategy and putting aside resources for growth with your board, not fundraising operations. Focusing on financial strategy is a better use of their time than wordsmithing an annual appeal. And more exciting for them.

Let them dream about what your agency can do in the community. Get them excited about future possibilities and teach them how to take that excitement into the community. Let them be the mission ambassadors they signed up to be instead of tying their hands with operations. Let them help you bring in the money by exciting your community. We spoke about planning for financial and mission growth in **Chapter Five**.

Of course, hiring a development director does not mean board members should think they're off the fundraising hook. They are not. As we pointed out earlier, fundraising is integral to board service. In fact, hiring a development director means that they will be more, not less, involved in fundraising than they were before. A good development director will work with the board to grow your donor base and create opportunities to spread your vision to the community. It is your board members who are your primary mission ambassadors.

Don't forget about bringing fundraising volunteers on board. In our next section, we explore how you can use volunteers in your fundraising program. We examine how to find good fundraising volunteers in **Chapter Twelve** and how to retain them in **Chapter Thirteen**.

Volunteers and Fundraising

The Corporation for National and Community Services reports that 25 percent of Americans ages 16 and older volunteer. According to Volunteer Hub, volunteers spend an average of fifty hours per year donating their time. More than 71 percent of volunteers work with only one organization per year. About 9 percent of volunteers engage in fundraising.

What Fundraising Volunteers Do

Fundraising volunteers can perform a variety of tasks including serving on the development committee, planning, and coordinating and implementing specific fundraising activities such as direct mail appeals, phone-a-thons, peer-to-peer campaigns, email campaigns, text-to-give appeals, business campaigns, in-person solicitations, special events, and capital campaigns.

Volunteers can also research community trends, business websites, grant prospects, and potential individual donors. You can have them gather secondary or primary data. If you want them to gather primary data, however, you must train them in how to do so.

You need community volunteers to sit on your development committee. You want their outside perspectives so they can guide you in reaching other community members. You also want as many hands-on-deck as you can get. Especially ones that you don't have to financially compensate. Volunteers need staff support, though. They should not replace needed staff.

What exactly your fundraising volunteers will do depends on the type of fundraising that is right for your organization. Fundraising endeavors that are right for your agency promote your nonprofit's mission, raise significant amounts of net income, appeal to your donors, and fit within your organization's capacity.

Getting the Most Out of Volunteers

Volunteers need to be managed and supported correctly. They, like staff, need role definition, including job descriptions and training. If you haven't already, implement an orientation and training program for your fundraising volunteers. Set up a leadership structure they can grow into as they seek greater challenges. Have them report to someone and meet with them to talk about performance. Hold them accountable for their actions and gently guide them when they stray. It will help your volunteer retention too. We talk about retaining volunteers in **Chapter Thirteen**.

Volunteers freely give their time and talent. You and your staff are grateful for the tasks they carry out, how they moderate your workload, and what they add to your resource base. People need to be validated for their contributions. Constantly thank your volunteers for what they do to help meet your nonprofit's mission. And publicly reward them for a job well done. Give them what they need to stay motivated.

The Chain of Command

Lines of communication and responsibility can be blurred as there are both board and staff members with positions of authority involved in your fundraising efforts. You, as executive director, may also be involved. How do you manage relationships when you direct the organization and staff, your development director is most knowledgeable about fundraising, and the board member development committee chair governs the agency?

My answer is to make roles clear during the recruitment and onboarding processes. And reinforce them continually. You want to make the board, staff, and volunteer experiences as smooth and enjoyable as you can so that your board members, satisfied employees, and volunteers become ambassadors for your organization and spread the word about your nonprofit further into the community.

The board member development committee chair leads and sets the tone for meetings and activities. The development director provides the expertise, organizational information, materials, and training for the fundraising volunteers. And the subcommittee chairs supervise the individual volunteers with the support of the development director.

An optimal reporting structure looks something like the following:

Full Development Committee Structure

Board Member Chair

Development Director

Fundraising Subcommitte 1 | Fundraising Subcommittee 2 | Fundraising Subcommittee 3 | Fundraising Subcommittee 4

Your job is to supervise the development director and work with your board chair to support the board liaison.

For a more detailed discussion about using volunteers in your fundraising program, see the ***Nonprofit Quick Guide: How to Involve Volunteers in Your Fundraising Program***.

Carlos' Solution

To get the most out of his fundraising staff investment, I suggested a team approach. He could hire a part-time, experienced development director who was a generalist. He could also hire a part-time administrative assistant to support both him and the incoming development director.

In the meantime, we would conduct an assessment of the organization's fundraising strengths and gaps. The data we gathered would shape the development plan that would subsequently be refined by the development director. At the same time, Carlos would work with the board to form a development committee. A board member liaison would lead the committee and the development director would provide staff support. The committee would begin operating once the development director was hired.

The board continued their ambassadorship to the community. As more and more community members became excited about what the nonprofit was doing, they were approached and asked how they would like to become involved. Since the board had set up a development committee and had job descriptions for interested fundraising volunteers, they were able to tell these potential volunteers what they needed them to do. Some said yes to becoming fundraising volunteers.

Carlos was on his way from going to almost no fundraising support to a robust fundraising team consisting of board members, a development director, and several fundraising volunteers. Now he had more than himself and a few board members raising money. The chances for financial success with more people involved increased dramatically from the original vision of one staff person raising all the money.

Wrapping It Up

The board's job in fundraising is to strategically allocate resources and monitor their acquisition. A development committee consisting of board members, staff, and fundraising volunteers serves as the bridge between the governance activities of the board and the operational activities of the staff.

Development committee responsibilities include proposing fundraising policies and procedures, developing the agency funding plan, overseeing fundraising activities, monitoring performance, evaluating results against the plan, and ensuring board involvement in fundraising. The board liaison leads and sets the tone for development committee meetings and activities. The development director provides the expertise, organizational information, materials, and training for the fundraising volunteers. And the subcommittee chairs supervise the individual volunteers with the support of the development director.

Plan for growth. Set aside a portion of overall surplus for growth. Build up your reserves through the financial efficiencies you incorporate into your fundraising plan.

As your fundraising program grows, hire enlightened generalists rather than traditional fundraising specialists. Putting the onus on generalist fundraisers to meet total donor needs enables you to build relationships with more donors with less resource investment. If you want your development director, donor relationship managers, and grant writer to carry out their responsibilities successfully, then hire administrative support for them. You want your fundraisers pursuing and procuring donations, not spending time tending to clerical details.

To afford experienced development professionals, considering hiring them part-time. Look at how you advertise the position, offer fair pay, and present exciting organization-shaping opportunities to attract staff that may otherwise overlook working for a small to midsized nonprofit.

Fundraising volunteers can perform a variety of tasks including serving on the development committee, research, planning, and coordinating and implementing specific fundraising endeavors. They freely give their time and talent, moderating your and your staffs' workload and adding to your nonprofit's resource base. Constantly thank your volunteers for their efforts and publicly reward them for a job well done. You want the volunteer experience to be as pleasing and satisfying as possible.

Points to Remember

- The board's job is to focus on governance and strategy and provide an environment that supports the executive director and staff in executing the strategies they have deemed most effective. The development committee brings together board, staff, and volunteers to achieve their mission and operational objectives.

- As your organization grows, instead of hiring traditional fundraising specialists, build a team with similar skills and complementary strengths. Structure your management matrix around donors' needs, not their method of gift giving.

- Volunteers give freely of their time and talent. They, like staff, need job descriptions, orientation, training, and supervision. To encourage long-term or serial involvement, create a leadership structure they can grow into.

What's Next

Once we structure our fundraising team, it is time to recruit them. **Chapter Twelve** delves into how to attract and recruit good board members, development professionals, and fundraising volunteers.

Chapter Twelve

Choose Your Pick

Hannah, the executive director of a community childcare agency serving low-income parents, needed more fundraising volunteers. Her development director was overloaded with work, inundated with tasks that could easily be delegated to someone else. But there was no money for additional staff. How could Hannah help her development director recruit the volunteer help she needed?

Fundraising and Recruitment

To excite your community to give—the fourth step of The Sustainable High ROI Fundraising System—you need strong team contributors. You need good board members, competent employees, and enthusiastic fundraising volunteers. Building a team like that starts with recruiting the right people. In this chapter, we address how to recruit outstanding board members, development professionals, and fundraising volunteers, including how to find them, interview questions to ask them, and how to ask them to be part of your organization.

Recruiting Good Board Members

Your board is the most valuable leadership asset your nonprofit has. Board members teach the community how to interact with your agency. And the board is where an infectious fundraising culture starts. It is imperative that you recruit board members thoughtfully and with intention.

Governance versus Management

To begin recruiting board members, you need to understand their role so that you can adequately communicate expectations and board members know what they are signing up to do. Many prospective board members think that they will be managing an agency. They will not—that's your job. They will be governing the agency, not managing it.

Governance is the strategic task of setting organizational goals, direction, limitations, and accountability frameworks. Management is the allocation of resources and overseeing the day-to-day operations

To realize the greatest efficiencies in fundraising, your board must understand how to set realistic financial goals, determine the overall revenue-generation direction, what the inherent limitations are, what other limitations they may want to implement, and how they will hold you accountable for meeting your financial goals.

Although you will be deciding the details of how funds are spent, your board will be involved in approving the budget. You need board members who understand their role in fundraising and are engaged in the process.

Profile of a Good Board Member

A good board member is committed to the cause. Provide opportunities for volunteers to be involved with your nonprofit and look for those who are dedicated and committed to your nonprofit's mission. A good proving ground for potential board members are committees and subcommittees where the community can be involved—perhaps on a development, volunteer, or marketing committee.

Clarifying Point

Profile of a Good Member

Committed
Leader
Good communicator
Inquisitive
Keeps confidences
Good character
Culture fit
Networked

You don't want just anybody on your board either. You want someone with leadership skills who can guide and influence others. It is important that board members be able to fulfill their role as mission ambassadors of the organization and can draw others in. Your goal is to grow your nonprofit's influence and impact in the community.

You also want to recruit people who are straightforward and impartial. As an executive director, you need strong board member support. And that starts with good communication. Start creating open lines of communication from the beginning. Choose people who will promote good communication and decision-making.

Look for people with an insatiable desire to learn, who are inquisitive, realizing that they do not know everything. You want people who are open to the ideas of others and will function as part of a team.

You also need board members who value discretion and confidentiality. This trait is particularly important when the organization is faced with delicate situations. You also want to build trust among board members.

Board members should be of good character, beyond reproach. You want to keep your nonprofit's good reputation intact.

To avoid unnecessary conflict, you want people who can fit into your agency's culture. You don't want a maverick who comes in with a mindset of automatically changing the way things are done. There is often good reason why things are done the way they are. Be cognizant of and communicate your organizational culture to board prospects.

And you want board members who are willing to use their personal and professional resources to advance the mission. This doesn't mean asking them to share their contact list with you. It means they need to be willing to make important connections that only they can make. Which means that connections are made deliberately and with forethought, not en masse.

Identifying Potential Board Members

In today's world, diversity, equity, and inclusion are ruling principles in board recruitment. You want diversity in all the ways your board can be diverse, including:

- Age
- Gender
- Ethnicity
- Ability/Disability
- Education
- Income
- Occupation
- Marital status
- Family makeup

Rather than recruiting your friends, family, and co-workers or those of your current board members to fill board vacancies, develop a matrix of the attributes desired in board members that reflects the makeup of your ideal board. Then fill in the matrix with current board membership information. What's missing describes the type of people you want to recruit for board service.

Hopefully you are not the one doing all this work. Ideally, your board committee structure includes a governance committee or nominating committee or subcommittee that does the bulk of the work. You need to be involved for sure. But it is the governance or nominating chair who takes the lead.

Always interview prospective board members—you and a member of the board. You want to make sure that the prospect is as good in person as on paper, interested in the job, capable of carrying out board member duties, and willing to take on the legal and fiduciary responsibilities of board membership.

Initially Approaching Potential Board Members

Just like with potential donors, the goal of your initial contact is not to get them to say 'yes'. Instead, the goal of your initial conversation is to connect, find information, and get a better understanding of one another. You start the recruitment process by building a relationship based on trust, respect, and mutual interest in furthering your organization's mission.

So, during the first interaction ask questions and listen more than you talk. The introductory meeting is not the time to promote your nonprofit. It is a time to learn more about them. Find out what makes them tick and what their values are. You want to connect with them on their values. Connecting with people on values builds camaraderie and a shared interest in success. That's a great foundation on which to build a board member-executive director relationship.

Listen, actively listen, to them. Active listening requires you to be wholly involved in and fully present for during the conversation. You pay attention to what the speaker is saying, verbally and nonverbally, not planning on what you're going to say next. During the interaction, face the potential board member and maintain eye contact. Focus entirely on what they are saying. Give them 100 percent of your attention. Get to know them. There will be time later for you to promote your nonprofit.

The Second Interaction

The goal of the second interaction is to assess board candidate's suitability and fit for board service at your nonprofit. Now is the time to introduce the particulars of your agency.

The Board Member Recruitment Packet

Create a recruitment packet to give to board prospects to help them understand your organization, their role as board member, and the required time and financial commitment. Your goal is to define expectations from the beginning.

Things to include in your board recruitment packet include:

- Board member job description
- Organizational mission, vision, and values statements
- Governance versus management piece
- Board organizational chart

- Names of other board members
- Articles of Incorporation
- IRS determination letter
- Bylaws
- Strategic plan
- Programming and impact statements
- Annual report

The Board Member Interview

Bring the packet with you to the interview. Be prepared to answer questions like:

- Who is on the board now and how did they got there?
- How long are the terms?
- How many people are required for a quorum?
- What committees exist? Who is on them?
- What do the financials look like?
- What is the annual operating budget?
- What are the responsibilities of board members?

Answer whatever questions they have. Be straightforward throughout the interview, including any challenges the organization is facing. Help them be fully aware of what they're getting into. Help them make an informed decision.

And ask them questions, too. Listen to their answers carefully. You are screening for the characteristics we described above. Sample questions include:

- Why are you interested in our organization?
- What do you know about us?
- What experience do you have related to our mission?
- What connections/contacts can you contribute?

- How much time can you contribute?
- What other resources can you contribute?
- What qualities make a good board member?
- What personal qualities can you bring to the board?
- What do you expect from our organization?
- What factors in your life might inhibit your ability to serve?
- How do you feel about performance evaluations?
- Will you feel comfortable conducting a self-evaluation?
- What motivates you as an individual?
- What role do you think you would play on the board?
- Would you be willing to attend a lunch with the executive director in which the goal was to ask for money?
- What do you know about the field?
- Do you have any questions for us?

Asking Board Members to Serve

When you ask prospects to serve on the board, again, be clear about what is expected of them and what they're getting into. And you shouldn't do the ask. A member of the governance committee should. Have them do their homework so they can communicate:

- Why the board exists
- How the board defines success
- When the board is of most value to the organization
- How the board functions as a group
- What individual behaviors the board values
- What outcomes are tracked
- The legal requirements that govern board members, including the duties of care, loyalty, and obedience

- The nonprofit's most significant risk
- How board members are protected from liability
- The nonprofit's financial position
- The nature of the board-executive director relationship
- Lines of communication and decision-making

Board membership is an awesome responsibility. And board leadership is crucial to fundraising success. Make sure you and your board put in the time and effort necessary to recruit well.

Recruiting Good Development Staff

Just as you want to recruit good members, you want to recruit competent staff. To do that, you must create an appealing job ad and distribute it where fundraising professionals will see it, facilitate a knockout interview, and make an appealing offer.

When you interview a development professional for a staff position, you are assessing fundraising and relationship-building abilities, determining culture fit, and setting expectations. Overall, you are looking for someone who:

- Is passionate about your mission
- Is passionate about their job
- Increases fundraising net income
- Will work well with you
- Will work well with board members
- Will work well with co-workers
- Will work well with volunteers
- Will work well with donors
- Is ethical

The Job Ad

A development director is a fundraising generalist with skills and experience in a wide variety of revenue generation activities. Their duties include managing donor relationships, interacting with donors to encourage giving, writing and submitting grant proposals, seeking out sponsorships, and executing fundraising events, depending on your agency's revenue mix. Sometimes they also have marketing and communication responsibilities. As your fundraising program grows, they will supervise other needed fundraising staff.

When you advertise for the job, highlight the things that will attract excellent fundraisers to the position. Underline the position's contribution to advancing your agency's mission. Talk about the working partnership with you and your board. Offer flexible work hours. Tell potential applicants about any continuing education opportunities that are provided.

To attract experience and know-how, set a slightly above average starting pay rate for your area. State the salary and benefits. Show your organization's diversity, equity, inclusion, and access initiatives. Declare that veterans, mothers, BIPOC, and people with disabilities are welcome and encouraged to apply.

And don't think you have to hire full-time. Experienced professionals can usually perform a task much more quickly than a novice and their learning curve is not as steep. As we talked about in **Chapter Eleven**, there are things other than money that will attract talent to your organization.

Share the opportunity where skilled fundraisers are likely to see it. List the job with groups and publications such as:

- Association for Fundraising Professionals, national and local chapters
- Grant Professionals Association
- Statewide associations of the National Council for Nonprofits
- Chronicle of Philanthropy

- Nonprofit Times
- Idealist
- LinkedIn
- Indeed
- Glassdoor

The Staff Interview

The role of the development director is to work with you to infuse a fundraising culture into your agency and work with you, board members, and volunteers to raise money. A development director oversees all of your fundraising efforts.

When you conduct job interviews with potential development staff, assess for soft skills including self-awareness, self-perception, confidence, motivation, determination, and tact. Look for relationship-building, analytical, problem-solving, and conflict resolution skills. Discover their knowledge of revenue streams and financial prowess.

Determine how they handle possible and actual failure. And get a sense of their priorities, such as what fundraising skills are most important to them and their priority on satisfying donors' and volunteers' needs. Explore their values, sense of personal responsibility, and adherence to ethical standards. You want to make sure their personal priorities and mindset will fit with your nonprofit's. You can also pick up on potential for longevity.

Questions that reveal these things include:

1. Tell me about yourself. *(You're assessing self-perception and confidence.)*

2. What is your greatest strength? *(You're assessing skill fit.)*

3. What is your biggest weakness? *(You're assessing self-awareness, skill, and organizational fit.)*

4. Why do you want this job? *(You're assessing motivation.)*

5. How has your experience prepared you for this role? *(You're assessing soft as well as hard skills.)*

6. What makes you uniquely qualified for this job? *(You want to see skill level, what fundraising skills are most important to them, outstanding relationship-building skills, and adherence to industry ethical standards.)*

7. How do you define fundraising success? *(You're looking for someone who puts a priority on raising money, satisfying volunteer needs, and satisfying donors' wants and needs.)*

8. How much money do you raise in a typical year? Is that net or gross revenues? *(You're looking for fundraising ability and financial prowess.)*

9. What kind of fundraising have you done in the past and how successful were you? *(You're looking for knowledge regarding diversity of revenue streams, skill attainment, and clues as to further training needs.)*

10. What professional accomplishment are you most proud of? *(You're assessing personal priorities and values.)*

11. Tell me about a time you overcame a fundraising challenge. *(You're looking for determination, tact, and how they interact with you, board members, co-workers, volunteers, and donors when faced with a possible failure.)*

12. Tell me about a time you failed to meet your financial goals. *(You're assessing how they handle failure personally, with you, fundraising volunteers, donors, co-workers, and board members.)*

13. Tell me why you think you failed to reach your financial goals. *(You're looking for analytical skills and sense of personal responsibility.)*

14. What would you do differently to reach your financial goals today? *(You're looking for problem-solving skills.)*

15. Tell me about a time you failed to meet your donor relationship goals. *(You're assessing how they handle failure personally, with you, and with donors.)*

16. Tell me why you think you failed to save or develop the relationship. *(You're looking for analytical skills and a sense of personal responsibility.)*

17. What would you do differently to keep the donor or move the donor up the ladder today? *(You're looking for problem-solving skills.)*

18. Tell me about how you work with board members. *(You're looking for a team mindset when working with you.)*

19. Tell me about a time you worked with a difficult board member. *(You're looking for conflict resolution skills.)*

20. Tell me about a time when you worked with a difficult donor. *(You're assessing tact and ability to satisfy donor needs and wants.)*

21. Tell me about a time you were recognized by your executive director for your work. *(You're seeing what previous supervisors valued in them.)*

22. Tell me about a time you worked hard, achieved your goal, and someone else got the credit. *(You're looking for a propensity toward teamwork.)*

23. Tell me about an ethical dilemma you had and how you handled it. *(You are looking for adherence to ethical standards.)*

24. What do you hope this job has that your last one didn't? *(You're assessing motivation and values.)*

25. What are your career goals? *(You're assessing possibility of longevity.)*

26. If you were hired, what might make you leave? *(You're looking for organizational fit and assessing potential for longevity.)*

27. Do you have anything else to tell me? *(You're assessing what else they think is important.)*

28. Do you have any questions for me? *(Listen to the questions they ask, evaluating skill level, values, priorities, and culture fit.)*

Industry Ethical Standards

It is unethical in the field to pay fundraisers a percentage of funds raised. I know a fair amount of salespeople are paid on a commission basis. In those cases, the companies' profits benefit the business owner(s), not the public. When the money goes for the inurement of the public, different standards apply. Payment of a percentage of fees given for the public good is not fair to all parties involved.

Because there are so many organizational factors out of their control—for example, the percentage of board giving or the financial position of the agency or political influences affecting donor decisions—the fundraiser deserves to be paid whether a donation goes through or not.

And the agency shouldn't have to pay a big chunk of revenues to fundraisers because of a big donation. Number one, that means money is not going towards mission, it's going to an individual. Nonprofits have a legal responsibility to use public funds for public benefit, not private inurement. Number two, the compensation may be above what the fundraiser is worth.

It's also not fair to the donor who donates to a cause, not a paycheck.

I know there are people who do it. Stay away from these people, It is unethical to pay fundraisers on a commission basis.

The Job Offer

When you present an offer, make sure to include the job title and description, exempt or non-exempt classification, name and position of their supervisor, salary, benefits, terms of employment, start date, basic work schedule, and any contingencies to employment such as background or reference checks in the letter. Give them an employee manual with all company policies. Unless the position is offered via a contract, have them sign a statement that they understand this is at-will employment. Have them also sign a confidentiality agreement and a non-compete clause.

Recruiting Good Fundraising Volunteers

Volunteers make up the third component of your fundraising team. And they need to be recruited with as much forethought as board members and employees.

Just as you do with prospective board members, you screen, interview, and assess fundraising volunteers before signing them on. And just like board members, you want to set expectations from the start. But where do you find all the volunteers you need? What questions should you ask them during an interview? And how do you get them to say 'yes?'

It's okay to have standards for volunteer involvement, especially when it comes to fundraising. Fundraising volunteers will be interacting with prospective donors and often have access to sensitive information. It is just as important that your fundraising volunteers have discretion, can keep confidentialities, and are of good character as it is your board members.

The Volunteer Recruitment Packet

In the same way you develop a board recruitment packet, you develop a fundraising volunteer recruitment packet. Items to include in your volunteer recruitment packet include:

- Job description
- Timeline
- Contact information for the person the volunteer will be reporting to
- Fundraising project organizational chart
- List of other volunteers working on the project
- Case for support
- Project budget
- Annual Report
- Programming and impact information

Your goals are to not only apprise the fundraising volunteers of the project, their roles in it, and their responsibilities as part of it, but to also let them see how what they will be doing contributes to mission fulfillment. Always remember that it is the mission that motivates. They are raising money to change people's lives and make the world a better place. Help them see how their volunteering meets that goal.

Identifying Fundraising Volunteers

Since it is the mission that motivates both volunteers and donors, identifying volunteers is similar to identifying donors. That is, the best fundraising volunteer prospects will have an interest in your mission, a connection to your agency, and the time to give to volunteering.

Connection

As we mentioned in **Chapter Ten**, connections to your agency include:

- Family members
- Friends
- Co-workers
- Fellow college alumni
- Fellow high school alumni
- Fellow civic group members
- Fellow house of worship attenders
- Fellow sports team members
- Parents of child's friends
- Service providers
- Social contacts

Once you have brainstormed a list of connections, write down what you already know about them. You will not approach all the people on your list to volunteer, though. In addition to a connection to your organization, volunteer prospects should exhibit interest in your cause and have the time to give.

Interest

When you contact a potential volunteer, note how you are received. People who are interested in what you have to say will generally greet you more warmly than those who don't. A cool reception, however, does not necessarily mean disinterest. The timing might not be right. If you do receive a cool reception, note it and, unless you get a firm 'no', follow up at a later time.

Also note the length of the conversations. Longer conversations generally indicate higher levels of engagement. In addition, rate the quality of the conversation and the prospect's interest in your cause and specific organization.

And follow up on any requests for more information or promises that you made.

Capacity

During the conversation, in addition to assessing their level of interest and enthusiasm, you will also be asking about the amount of time they have to give. And how much of that time they want to devote to volunteering for your nonprofit. The number of hours they have to give can range from one or two hours a year to nine to ten hours a week. They may also be able to serve during only certain times of the year. Knowing their time constraints will help you determine what kinds of fundraising support they can give to your agency and what type of roles they can take on.

The Volunteer Interview

Interview potential volunteers in the same way you interview board prospects. Questions to ask people interested in volunteering for your nonprofit include:

1. What are your interests?

2. What skills do you bring with you?

3. What skills do you hope to acquire?

4. What do you hope to gain from your volunteer experience?

5. How does this commitment fit in with all your other commitments?

6. How much time do you have?

7. How much flexibility do you want?

8. Do you want to work alone or in a group?

9. What kind of assignment to you want—ongoing, short-term, long-term, or one-time?

10. How long do want the assignment to be?

Not only do you assess for role assignment, you also assess for training needs. Because volunteers want and need training. They aspire to do a good job. Help them achieve their goal.

Asking Volunteers to Serve

The key to getting potential volunteers to say 'yes' is to give them amazing opportunities to make a difference. Remember, it is the mission that motivates. Help them see the big picture by showing them how their work relates to fulfilling your agency's mission.

And communicate, communicate, communicate. As with board members, let them know exactly what they're getting into. Be open, honest, and forthright. Let them know the good and not so good so they know what to expect.

Don't waste their time or yours. Recognize when a situation is a no-go. Sometimes you can't offer what they want. And that's okay. You do not need to accept a donation of time just because it is offered.

If the engagement is a go, connect with them on a personal level. Don't only see them as task doers. Volunteers appreciate a personal touch.

And then welcome them to the team as part of the family.

Hannah's Solution

Hannah took her development director aside and asked her to brainstorm requirements of all fundraising volunteers, regardless of position. She also asked her to create job descriptions for the different types of work she could delegate to volunteers. Hannah took what her development director had done and asked her to include the agency's current case for support, promotional materials, and annual report and created fundraising recruitment packets.

Hannah then asked the program volunteers, board members, and the rest of the staff if they had any connections who would be interested in volunteering to help with fundraising for the agency. The development director subsequently contacted them to assess fit and availability. She arranged more time with those who were interested.

After the second interaction, prospective fundraising volunteers were invited to a development committee meeting where they could meet the rest of the team, get a real look at what was going on at the agency, and ask more questions. After attendance at the development committee meeting, prospects were asked how they would like to be involved.

Some of them realized that they would prefer volunteering on the program side of things. And some of them decided the development committee was how they could best contribute. The development director finally had some relief.

Wrapping It Up

Just as you recruit staff, it is important to recruit board members and fundraising volunteers with intention. All three constituencies should be screened, interviewed, and assessed before they are asked to become part of the agency. For your fundraising to be successful, candidates must fit into your organizational culture and understand the expectations surrounding their roles. They will all, at one point or another, be interacting with donors, sometimes with access to sensitive information. It is important that your whole team—board members, development staff, and fundraising volunteers—are of good character, have discretion, and can keep confidentialities.

Your board's governance or nominating committee will take the lead in identifying and recruiting new board members. To fill vacancies, determine what you and they want the makeup of their ideal board to look like, see where the holes are, and recruit to fill the holes. Create a recruitment packet that helps potential board members understand your agency, their role as a board member, and the commitments involved in serving. Be open with prospects, sharing both the good and the not so good about your nonprofit. When they are asked to serve, reiterate expectations.

To fill a fundraising staff vacancy, highlight the position's contribution to mission fulfillment, working partnership with the executive director, flexible work schedule, continuing education opportunities, and diversity, equity, inclusion, and access initiatives. When you conduct the job interview, look for relationship-building, analytical, problem-solving, and conflict resolution skills; fundraising expertise and performance; and their priorities, values, sense of personal responsibility, and adherence to ethical standards. When you present the offer, have them sign a confidentiality agreement and non-compete clause.

Look for fundraising volunteers who have an interest in your mission, a connection to your agency, and the time to give to volunteering. Create a fundraising volunteer recruitment packet that describes the fundraising project they will be involved in, their roles and responsibilities, and how they will be contributing to mission fulfillment. When you interview potential volunteers, assess their skills, interests, time availability, and training needs. If they are a fit, help volunteers say "yes" by giving them amazing opportunities to make a difference. Remember, it is the mission that motivates.

Points to Remember

- Whether you are recruiting board members, development staff, or fundraising volunteers, define expectations from the beginning.

- When you interview prospective board members, staff, or fundraising volunteers, be specific about the state of your nonprofit, flow of information, their roles, and what commitments they are making.

- Show board members, staff, and volunteers how their work relates to fulfilling your agency's mission. Let them see how they are changing people's lives and making the world a better place.

- Always be straightforward, open, honest, and forthright with prospective members of your fundraising team.

What's Next

You don't want to go to all the trouble of recruiting your dream team only to have them resign and move on. You want to keep what you've got. You want to realize a high return on all that investment. Plus, you want to keep up the relationships that have been built between dream team members and your donors. Read on to hear how to retain the human investments you have made in your fundraising, that is, bringing on board good board members, staff, and volunteers.

Chapter Thirteen

Keep What You've Got

M aria, executive director of a maternal and health agency, knew she had to do something. She had just lost her development director. Important work was not going to get done until she could find a replacement. The turnover was a heavy drain on resources. Maria couldn't move her fundraising to where she wanted it to be without staff help. The next time she hired, she wanted to make sure her development professional stayed.

Invest in Retention

It pays to invest in retention. It takes a lot of time to build your perfect team of board members, employees, and volunteers. Turnover costs take away from the bottom line, not only in terms of dollars and cents, but also the organizational relationships that have been built. And it is within the context of satisfying relationships that money is raised. A loss in time, money, and relationship building is a triple whammy. You want to avoid it at all costs. To help you keep what you've worked so hard to achieve, this chapter is devoted to helping you realize a high return on the investment it took to build your fundraising team.

Retaining Good Board Members

Your board members are the community leaders of your agency. You put a lot of energy into developing relationships with board members. You want to get the most you can from those relationships for as long as you can. Which means working with your board chair to provide a good board experience, onboarding new board members correctly, training them, providing them with meaningful work, and evaluating their performance.

The Board Chair Role

Simply put, the board chair manages the board while you manage the staff. As such, it is the board chair's role to ensure board member expectations are discussed and agreement is reached. And the board chair is responsible for creating the environment in which board members work. The chair may have help, for example through the executive committee and/or a governance committee. But ultimately it is the board chair who ensures that the work of the board is done.

And then there is you. Although you will have relationships with every board member, and your development director may too, it is the board chair who you will turn to in matters regarding board member behavior and performance. You and your board chair work in tandem to make sure things runs smoothly.

Onboard Correctly

If you want a high-functioning board, you need to discuss expectations from the beginning. We talked about recruiting good board members in the last chapter. The next step is to onboard them.

One of the easiest ways to reinforce board roles is to create a board member binder for each new board member. The binder should include, at a minimum, a:

- Board list with contact information and terms of service
- Board member job description
- Brief definition of governance with agency examples of how governance differs from management
- The legal and fiduciary responsibilities of board members
- Previous year's board minutes
- Board and board member evaluation forms

- Current year agency budget
- Financial statements
- Their signed commitment to the terms of their board service, including a conflict-of-interest statement

When you give them their binder, go over it with them. Do not leave it up to them to review the material. You want to give them time to ask you questions and build a relationship with you. You want to engage them even further than they are.

You also want them to meet one-on-one with the board chair. You want a peer-to-peer, volunteer-to-volunteer exchange. If you and the board president are working as a team, the expectations you outlined will be reinforced during that meeting. Plus, another relationship will start to bud, strengthening the connection between the new board member and your organization.

Match your board member with a board colleague as a mentor or decide on one before the new member's first meeting. Broaden the board relationships you create. Use the power of group connection to invest board members in their service.

As social creatures, people want to feel part of a team. So, get new board members on a committee or project right away. Let them feel a part of things. Help them feel needed and important. Use their talents. Give them opportunities to see how they contribute to the agency's wellbeing. Motivate them to stay,

In addition, conduct three-, six-, nine-, and twelve-month check ins, just to see how things are going. Continue to solidify your relationship with them. You also want to know about and correct any misconceptions that have formed. Your purpose is to reinforce expectations while ensuring a positive, satisfying board experience.

Provide Training

It is board members who teach the community how to interact with the nonprofit they represent. They set the example. And they need training on how to do that. Don't set your board members up to feel like failures—help them succeed. Invest in regular, ongoing board training. We address training and development in **Chapter Fourteen**.

Offer Meaningful Work

One of the best tactics to encourage continued board service is to provide interesting and meaningful work. This means you focus on your nonprofit's mission and the strategies board members are taking to fulfill and grow it, not the tasks required to execute that strategy. Completing tasks in and of themselves does not lead to feeling a part of a larger purpose. There may or may not be anything exciting about them. Seeing progress toward meeting goals, on the other hand, is motivating. It shows people how what they do fits into the big picture. It gives them a sense of purpose.

You want to highlight your organization's impact. Because every step of your agency's progress in advancing its mission leads to more changed lives. Which gives their board service purpose. You want them excited about what they have accomplished so they will want to continue doing it.

It is thrilling to see board members doing what they signed up to do—advancing your nonprofit's mission. And you are making it a rewarding experience they want to keep doing. How great is that?

Evaluate Performance

What gets measured gets done. Every board should have goals they are striving to reach. Governance goals, that is. We gave a list of questions should be asking about fundraising in **Chapter Three** including:

- Are we fulfilling our duties to provide resources to implement and grow our mission?

- Do we have a written strategic plan that we regularly review and update?

- Are we constantly promoting mission in all we do, even in our fundraising strategy?

- Have we provided a favorable environment for the executive director and staff to succeed in raising money? For example, do we have written board giving and gift acceptance policies in place that we enforce?

- Are we making progress in meeting our mission and financial goals?

Regular evaluation is how you answer them.

Board members should also be aware of how they are functioning as a group. Evaluation is how they determine whether their group dynamics are healthy or not.

Individually

People want feedback. They want to be recognized for their contributions. And they need to be alerted when their behavior is disruptive, divisive, or inappropriate or when they are not abiding by their commitments.

It is the board chair's job to make sure such conversations are held. And the board as a whole to enforce adherence to agreed-upon expectations. Your role under these circumstances is to support board members in any way you can and let board leaders take care of the issue.

Corporately

The board as a whole also needs feedback. Best practices are they conduct an annual evaluation, so they are aware of how well they are functioning as a group. The standards can be set by the governance or executive committee. Board members can then use the feedback to improve performance and determine training needs. A quick internet search can uncover a multitude of resources to help boards conduct self-evaluations.

Express Gratitude

Thank your board members for their work on the organization's behalf. It isn't easy being a board member, especially a chair. They need support and encouragement just as much as you do. Plus, how you treat people is generally how they will treat you. Treat all board members, no matter how much they drive you crazy, with respect, patience, and constant gratitude. A genuine thank you goes a long way to keeping board members on board.

Retaining Good Development Professionals

Not only do you want to retain good board members, you also want to retain good development staff. Which is not an easy job. The average tenure for a fundraising professional at the time of publication is fourteen months. According to a recent study by the Association of Fundraising Professionals, half of fundraisers surveyed reported that they intend to leave their jobs in the next two years.

When a development director leaves, not only do you incur turnover costs, you may also lose revenue. Your nonprofit's relationship with its donors may be at risk because maintaining relationships takes time and a fundraising vacancy means there is one less person to put the time into maintaining them. Retaining good development staff is key to successfully raising money.

Development professionals leave their jobs and look for new ones because:

1. They don't feel supported.

2. The culture is toxic.

3. There is little or no organizational infrastructure to facilitate philanthropy.

To avoid the revolving development professional door, onboard and orient new staff correctly, help them be successful, provide flexible hours, set reasonable goals, form a partnership with them, build a culture of philanthropy, let them know you appreciate their efforts, provide professional development opportunities, reward them, and show them how they can advance in their scope of responsibility.

Onboard and Orient

Have your development staff become familiar with your strategic plan. It is a blueprint for where your agency is going and how your agency will get there. And the development plan will be an offshoot of it.

Set aside time to define your fundraising staffs' roles in meeting the goals and objectives outlined in the strategic plan. Define your level of involvement with donors early on so your development director understands how the lines of communication with important constituencies will flow. Reinforce the fundraising roles and lines of communication between you and board members, the development director and board members, and you and the development director.

Set Your Staff Up for Success

Set your development staff up for success. When you articulate your fundraising goals, don't base them on a budget deficit or arbitrary percentage increases. Don't motivate your staff to leave by creating impossible goals. Communicate specific, measurable, action-oriented, realistic, and time-bound objectives based on forethought.

So that your nonprofit realizes a surplus, budget for a surplus. Focus on net, not gross, income. Include total, not just direct costs, in your calculations so you know exactly how much you need to raise. Make sure your fundraiser feels like they are reaching the goals that move the organization forward. You want to avoid them feeling stuck.

You also want to compare the financial returns of each fundraising activity you are considering. Focus your efforts on those activities with the highest return on investment. By doing so, you will expend the least amount of resources to achieve your goals, reducing your overall fundraising costs. And your development staff will feel a sense of accomplishment.

Clarifying Point

Do your homework and run your numbers. Set your development staff up for financial success.

Remember your revenue mix, though. It's not all about financial return on investment. The purpose of fundraising activities includes more than financial goals. Mission promotion and relationship building are also important considerations. Evaluate total success, that is, mission fulfillment, financial performance, and strengthening important relationships.

Come from a mission mindset. It is the mission that inspires people to give and the fulfillment of the mission that motivates people to give again. The best fundraisers are organizational ambassadors who talk about their agencies' missions and mission impact. Provide that mindset for them.

Give fundraising staff a complete organizational picture. Fundraising touches many organizational units including program, finance, planning, marketing, communications, IT, and board relations. Build strong interdepartmental teams, as we talked about in **Chapter Five**.

Provide Flexible Hours

Fundraising is not a nine to five job. Development professionals shouldn't be expected to punch a time clock. There are early morning business meetings to attend, evening networking events to participate in, and evening and weekend fundraisers to oversee. Plus, development staff have families. Expecting them to work constant sixty-hour weeks just to be in the office during all office hours is simply too demanding for most fundraising professionals. They, like you, need flexibility in their schedules to meet all their life responsibilities.

Set Reasonable Goals

Don't base your fundraising goals on a budget deficit, an arbitrary increase, salary costs, or what another nonprofit has been able to raise. To come up with a reasonable number, look at several years of your fundraising results and analyze the trends. Account for external economic conditions, too. You may want to grow exponentially, but what really is realistic, given the current state of affairs?

You must also account for the limitations of your nonprofit's infrastructure. How much your fundraising staff can raise is heavily influenced by the state of your infrastructure, including the level of your nonprofit's awareness in the community, agency's reputation, level of board giving, capabilities of your donor software, past upkeep of your donor database, quality of your case for support, number of donors, donor retention efforts, strength of your volunteer leadership, number of active fundraising volunteers, availability of administrative support, and so on. The list is endless. Account for the limitations you have when you set your fundraising goals. Set your staff up for success, not failure.

Form a Partnership

Fundraising touches almost all parts of a nonprofit: program, finance, IT, marketing, communications, volunteer training and management, and board relations. As such, fundraising staff members work most efficiently when they are aware of changes within your agency. They also perform most effectively when they are aware of the total needs of the organization so that they can direct energies toward securing the resources that best meet those needs.

Also, share what is going on within your agency partnerships, including your vendor relationships. A good fundraiser will go after any business or professional contacts that are candidates to be potential donors. Which is, at first, everyone your nonprofit has a relationship with. You want to make sure you present a consistent front to these contacts. For example, you don't want a potential wealthy business donor to be asked for a low donation. Nor do you want your development staff to approach a vendor with whom you have terminated a relationship. I've seen both happen.

Although your fundraising staff are responsible for implementing specific fundraising activities, you also bear some responsibility for how well your development staff performs. You, the executive director, set the tone, providing the environment your development staff operate in to raise the financial support needed for the agency to thrive and grow. Both of you deal with the external environment. Both engage in some of the same tasks, just at different levels, such as planning, budgeting, and evaluating. Both are dependent on one another to ensure success.

Ensure a Culture of Philanthropy

It is not your staff fundraising for your organization; it is them fundraising *with* everyone who is a part of your organization. Development professionals do not want to be lone rangers. There is a lot out of their control. They need support. They work better if they are part of one big team.

As the leader of the team, you need to set an example. Which means you need to give at a financial level significant for you. As do your board members. As leaders of the organization, you and your board model how you want the public to interact with you.

Fundraising is about getting people so excited about your cause they want to be part of it and make a donation because they know they can make a difference through your agency. It's about furthering a cause and making an important impact. Anyone involved with your nonprofit can do that. There is no right or wrong way to share passion for an important cause. So, tap into people's passion for your cause.

That means having your mission take a prominent place in your board meetings and volunteer trainings. Schedule a moment for mission. Have a recipient of your services come to tell the group how their life was changed by interacting with your nonprofit. Or let group members tell the others why they become involved with the agency in the first place. Make your mission real for them again. Remind them of why they do what they do so they can share with those outside the organization and get them excited about joining the team.

Appreciate a Job Well Done

When you give praise, don't just give general "good job" praise. Give specific thanks for a particular accomplishment. For example, "Thank you for speaking with Mr. Jones. He is an important community leader with a lot of influence. By introducing him to the work of our nonprofit, you paved the way for us to have lunch together. Now he's interested in donating to our cause and getting some of his contacts involved, too." Specific praise tells an employee you are aware of their actions and appreciate their good work. And they know they made a valuable contribution to the agency.

Offer Professional Development Opportunities

You want your development staff to grow and develop so they realize efficiencies in their work and pick up advanced fundraising skills. Provide professional memberships to your staff. Budget for them. Give your staff time to attend meetings. There they can network with other fundraisers who can help them solve a vexing problem, give them that next great fundraising idea, or support them in their work. They may even be able to find a mentor who can help them navigate the fundraising process. We talk more about professional development in the next chapter.

Offer fair pay increases.

One way to keep good fundraising staff is to financially reward them by linking raises and bonuses to performance, i.e., giving merit bonuses rather than cost-of-living increases. Just make sure that their performance exceeds agreed-upon goals. And are more than financial, including things like strengthening donor relationships, working with colleagues, and working with you and the board. You do not in any way want to appear that you are paying them a percentage of funds raised. You can also tie raises to overall agency financial success, as long as the board adopts a fair payment plan well in advance. For example, when the organization realizes a net surplus, a pre-determined amount of the proceeds is distributed to staff. Or you can base pay increases on a combination of individual merit and overall agency success. Just as long as it is not or does not appear to be a commission. Remember, it is unethical in the field to pay fundraisers a percentage of funds raised.

Show Them a Career Path within Your Agency

A career path does not necessarily mean there has to be a change in title. It may just mean a growth in responsibilities and pay. For example, a development director may always keep the title development director, but they may move up to supervise other fundraising staff. Or, as your development director becomes proficient at implementing one form of fundraising, they add another.

Say they are proficient in obtaining major gifts, you see this, and add more planned gift responsibilities to their job description. Of course, with the corresponding pay increase. And the corresponding help. Job descriptions can't just be growing without the needed support behind it.

Just like every other employee, a development director does not want to stay in a dead-end job that has no challenge for them anymore. Nor do you want someone who is bored with their job, unable to show enthusiasm for what they do anymore, representing your nonprofit to important others. This means you need to communicate your plans and priorities for growth to them.

Let your staff know where you want to take them. Be upfront with them. Let them know there is a future ahead for them that is not same old, same old. Give them a reason to stay.

Retaining Good Fundraising Volunteers

Not only do you want to retain good board members and development staff, you also want to retain good volunteers. Retaining fundraising volunteers employs many of the same tactics used to retain board and staff members.

Make volunteer retention a priority from the start, building it into your volunteer program, much like you integrate data collection into your programming. Create a deliberate retention strategy for your volunteer training program when you are designing it.

Food for Thought

You employ many of the same tactics to retain good board members, development staff, and fundraising volunteers.

Like board and staff members, volunteers should have job descriptions that clearly define work expectations. You should review these requirements before the volunteer signs on.

And then onboard them correctly. Like board members, get volunteers engaged and get involved immediately. Pair them up with a mentor or buddy. And get them working.

Be realistic about your expectations. Volunteers are not staff members. And they come with all kinds of skills and experiences. Invest time in training them. Train them in what you want you want them to do.

Be social and get to know them personally. Get to know your volunteers' values. Respect their values. And respect their time. Don't keep them waiting or just doing busy work.

Provide the resources they need to successfully accomplish their tasks. For example, scripts for making donor calls, limited authority to purchase items needed for events, or access to a research database. Be accessible to them so they know they have someone to turn to.

Ask them for their feedback about their roles. Think about new ways to communicate gratitude to them, enhance their experiences, and reward them. Continually thank them.

If you say you're going to do something, do it. Follow through is important.

Supervise your volunteers just as you do staff. Assess their performance and give feedback regularly. Let them know you appreciate a job well done.

Recognize your volunteers and their achievement in advancing the mission. Articulate the impact they are making, not only in terms of task completion but also in term of mission fulfillment. Remember, it is the mission that motivates. Always emphasize mission fulfillment. It is what your volunteers signed on for.

Maria's Solution

Maria wondered what she could do to help retain her next development director. She started by assessing her leadership style and outlining the type of relationship she wanted to have with her development director. She decided she was going to talk about the kind of working relationship she wanted during the job interview.

Next, Maria looked at the financial expectations for the job. Maria was getting pressure from some board members to keep those goals, but Maria wondered if they were reachable. She decided that she would hire an experienced development director who could help her answer that question.

One obstacle Maria felt she was up against was the low pay that went with the job. She decided to add a little to the salary line, hire part-time, and cut costs elsewhere so she could get the experience she needed. She also was going to be transparent about the budget situation with whomever was coming in. She couldn't promise a high starting salary or full-time work, but she could promise an ongoing investment in fundraising commensurate with the budget performance.

One plus she had going for her was that Maria did not care about keeping nine-to-five hours as long as the work got done. She would make sure to communicate that to interviewees.

Maria did find a new development director. And that development director has been with the agency for ten years now.

Wrapping It Up

To retain good board members, provide a good board experience. Discuss expectations and responsibilities up front. Have new board members meet with the president. Have the president assign them a mentor and get them involved right away. Facilitate a mid-year check in to see how it's going.

Provide board members with training. Offer meaningful work that focuses on the mission and strategies to advance it. Let board members see the impact they are making. Have your board chair facilitate regular board evaluations. And continuously express your gratitude to all board members for their service.

To retain development staff, give them direction, delineate lines of communication, and discuss your working relationship, making expectations clear. Set them up for success through your resource investments. Provide flexible work hours. Set reasonable goals. Don't base fundraising goals on a budget deficit, arbitrary increase, salary cost, or another nonprofit's results.

Form a partnership with your development director, sharing the state of the agency with them and apprising them of any changes. Build a culture of philanthropy with them. Appreciate a job well done. Offer professional development opportunities. Provide fair pay increases and show them how they can continue to develop in their position.

To retain fundraising volunteers, provide job descriptions and onboard them correctly. Set realistic expectations and discuss them upfront. Give them meaningful work, emphasizing its mission fulfillment and impact. Provide them with the resources necessary to complete their tasks. Follow through with what you said you would. Supervise them, continually evaluating them and providing them constructive feedback. Recognize and reward their efforts. And constantly thank them for their service. No one has ever been offended by being genuinely thanked too much.

Points to Remember

- Furnish new board members, staff, and volunteers with job descriptions and discuss them. Talk about expectations up front.

- Have realistic expectations of board members and volunteers. Set reasonable goals for staff performance.

- Offer mentoring programs for board members and volunteers. Get them involved in committee or project work right away.

- Provide meaningful work to board members and volunteers, emphasizing their roles in mission fulfillment and impact.

- Constantly thank board members, staff, and volunteers for their service. Recognize jobs well done.

What's Next

Ensuring training and professional development opportunities is a recurring theme when it comes to retaining board members, staff, and volunteers. While many nonprofits understand the importance of investing in continual education, many of them underinvest. The next chapter explores the returns on your investment in training and professional development, what fundraising skills you want your team to hone, and strategies for affording it,

Chapter Fourteen

Cultivate Brilliance

M att, executive director of a homeless services training agency, needed to step up his game. He had just gotten a big federal grant to increase the capacity of the area's homeless shelters, including their ability to attract their own funding. The grant had been written and submitted before Matt could inform the homeless shelters he worked with he was even applying. Now it was a matter of finding willing partners and executing the trainings he was granted funds to provide.

The hard part was not going to be finding willing partners or delivering services. The hard part was going to be helping these shelters realize the importance of ongoing training and getting buy-in to financially support ongoing training efforts.

Matt took a deep breath. He had a lot of work to do.

The Sustainable High ROI Fundraising System and Professional Development

Implementing The Sustainable High ROI Fundraising System involves empowering your board and mobilizing your staff and volunteers to fundraise. Training not only gives your team the skills they need to do their jobs better, it also communicates to them that you value their contributions so much you are willing to invest in developing them.

Most of your board members probably think fundraising is all about the asking. They do not truly understand the basis of fundraising. Therefore, they shy away from fundraising and are not skilled in its art.

Your staff and volunteers carry out fundraising operations. Your development director may or may not have additional responsibilities pertaining to marketing and communications. Your staff and volunteers may or may not have had formal training in what they're being asked to do, particularly if they are new to the field or have marketing and grant management responsibilities. Or they may know how to ask for money, but not be aware of all the nuances involved.

Providing training opportunities advances your nonprofit's growth. This chapter looks at the returns an investment in professional development produces, the skills your team needs to be successful, and how you can find the money for the continuing education.

Why Invest Heavily in Professional Development?

You want your team—board members, staff, and fundraising volunteers—to grow and develop by offering continuing education. And the reasons are many, including:

- It creates a culture of lifelong learning and continuous improvement.

- It increases engagement with your agency.

- It lets team members discover their passions and align them with their fundraising duties, creating a sense of purpose, increasing motivation, and decreasing attrition.

- It promotes awareness and an opportunity to hone team members' strengths.

- It boosts cognitive functioning.

- Your team will stay up to date with emerging technologies that can improve workflow, improving return on human investment.

- Your team will pick up advanced skills and perform their fundraising tasks more accurately and efficiently, reducing costs.

- Your staff will realize efficiencies in their work, increasing productivity. A Garter Research Study found that for every hour spent in employee training, five hours of productivity are saved annually.

- It improves morale by showing team members you value their contributions and expertise.

- It makes your nonprofit attractive to the others you want to get involved with your organization.

Any investment you make in training and professional development pays off in spades.

Increasing Hard Skills

Of course, you want to improve your team's hard skills, those technical proficiencies that help board members, staff, and volunteers better perform their tasks. For example, you may want to train board members in best practices in governance, understanding financial statements, strategic planning, legal responsibilities, and so forth. You may also want to hold specialized trainings for your committee and subcommittee chairs, for example, on how to facilitate a meeting.

You also want to encourage staff development through continuing education. Many fundraisers learn by doing and, therefore, have skill sets limited to their experience. Training in different forms of fundraising and the cadre of possibilities to execute a strategy is often helpful. Even fundraisers who have been around a while find additional training helpful if they have a specialized area of expertise and want a broader skill set to take on more leadership responsibilities.

As I pointed out in **Chapter Eleven**, I recommend hiring enlightened generalists to manage a specific group of donors who give gifts in all forms rather than hire specialists who are proficient in one form of fundraising. You can better meet the total needs of your donors by organizing your staff structure around them rather than their form of giving. Encourage a generalist understanding through your investment in professional development. Help your staff be who you want them to be. For example, fund staff pursuit of professional fundraising certifications, pay for industry workshops and conferences, and/or reimburse tuition for college and university classes. You need to set monetary limits, for sure. Just budget something, even if it is only paid time to attend.

Volunteers need training too. They need instruction in how to perform their tasks so that the donor experience is consistent between volunteers and over time. You also want to make sure that the data you need is collected and recorded consistently. You need to be able to compare apples to apples when you run reports. Again, you need consistency between people and over time.

Most volunteer training will be conducted in-house, whereas most staff training will be provided by outside organizations and board training by consultants.

Advancing Soft Skills

Hard skills are important to acquire. However, soft skills may be even more crucial to effective fundraising, because it is so relationship driven. A good fundraiser must be able to deal with all kinds of people with all kinds of backgrounds, perspectives, personalities, political viewpoints, values, and beliefs. The number one soft skill you want to hone is relationship-building. If a person can successfully build strong relationships, they can successfully raise money.

You also need to provide training in advanced communication skills. Communication skills are critical to fundraising, especially active listening, as we talked about in **Chapter Nine**. Good oral communication skills are important in face-to-face interactions, when you or your development staff are training volunteers, running staff and committee meetings, meeting with donors, or attending events. Writing skills are a must for submitting proposals, crafting appeals, creating marketing and promotional materials, and generating narrative reports. I'm sure you can think of hundreds of other ways honing good communication skills leads to better fundraising results.

Planning skills are a must, especially for an enlightened generalist who will have a multitude of priorities to juggle and tasks to complete. Good planning skills are also crucial when implementing special events with their many logistics to coordinate. Any tools that will help you and your staff plan ahead will make life easier for all parties. It will be easier to create and abide by a budget too.

Time management skills are essential to getting it all done. When I was a young fundraiser in the field many moons ago, the agency I was working for required me to attend a Franklin Covey seminar in calendaring and managing my time. I have been thankful ever since. Not that I still use the Franklin Covey system to a T, but I still use its principles and have adapted the techniques to fit my current day needs. I highly recommend that busy staff and executive directors avail themselves to the time management training and tools available to them. I usually find trainings in time management through corporate training firms.

> **Food for Thought**
>
> Hone communication, planning, time management, and negotiating skills. They are critical to garnering multiple donations from donors.

Negotiating skills are crucial, especially in asking for large personal gifts. Fundraising is a process where all parties come to agreement about the size, form, and timing of their donations. An effective fundraiser will be able to tap into an overarching goal, mission advancement, and negotiate these kinds of details. Realizing large gifts requires an open mind and a give and take of what you want and what the donor wants to do. Some of the most helpful books I have read were about negotiation. Usually, you find these books within the conflict resolution realm of topics. Sales courses also help develop competency in negotiation skills.

Read a book, attend a workshop, take a class, join a professional association, or find a mentor. Do what you and your team need to do to strengthen your relationship-building, communication, planning, time management, and negotiation skills. It will help your organization see increases in funding.

Affording Professional Development

Professional development is as much of a core cost as finance and human resources are. When you are building your budget, make professional development a priority. It makes no sense to spend money on hiring extra staff when you can realize the same benefit by improving efficiencies in your current staffing. Add staff only when efficiencies in current staffing cannot be realized.

Look at the financial and human return on investment. The results far exceed your costs. Run your numbers—the cost of status quo versus the cost of doing it more efficiently. To get the budget allocation from board members, create a chart demonstrating the financial effects of choosing the continuing education investment over the cost of things remaining the same. Run the numbers. Put it in terms of dollars and cents.

Plot out how you're going to fund professional development initiatives. Talk with your board about putting aside resources for staff, volunteers, and their growth. Plan how you're going to move ahead. We talked about planning for growth in **Chapter Five**.

To generate needed revenues, align your fundraising plan with your organizational budget. You want your fundraisers to be aware of agency training needs so they can find donors for it. Or negotiate for it. Or find volunteers to help deliver it. Make finding resources that help cover your professional development expenses a priority. Allocate time for it, collect data on finding and obtaining it, and measure results.

If you don't think you can find the funds, you may need to kill your scarcity mindset. As we talked about in **Chapter Four**, if you don't think you can raise the money, you probably won't. Your mindset has a lot to do with your success.

If you do need to cut costs, think seriously about whether or not you should cut your professional development costs. Because monies spent on training reduce overall costs and realize such a high return on investment.

Matt's Solution

Matt needed to find area homeless shelters willing to work with him on increasing capacity to pay for ongoing training after the federal grant he received ended. Finding agencies willing to sign up for the initial training was easy—they were all interested in what they could get for free. It was another story when it came to paying for training after the grant ended.

Matt worked with three agencies that bought into continuing professional education after the grant ended. They all understood the benefits of doing so, and were willing to make an investment in it.

Matt worked with each executive director to identify the training needs of each agency. He then researched what resources were available to provide those trainings, including his agency's, and how much they would cost. Because there were multiple agencies, Matt was able to negotiate group rates for some of the trainings. He also knew of area volunteer programs who could help deliver others.

Next, Matt researched and compiled a list of possible ongoing funding sources, including grants, corporate sponsorships, and large personal gifts. Since some of these donors were interested in area-wide initiatives, Matt formed a coalition of which he and each agency was a member. Just as Matt was able to negotiate group costs, he was able to negotiate group revenues.

Each executive director added the training costs into their budget. Matt gave them language they could use with board members, including graphs and charts that demonstrated the trainings' high return on investment.

Within a year, Matt was able to increase funding 25 percent over what it had been before.

Wrapping It Up

Providing training opportunities builds a culture of continuous improvement; increases staff engagement and motivation; improves morale; and decreases turnover. It hones team members' strengths and boosts their cognitive functioning, helping them perform better. Training helps your team stay abreast of new technologies and pick up advanced skills so they can improve their workflow, increase their productivity, and complete tasks more accurately. Providing professional development opportunities also helps attract qualified staff.

Improving hard skills helps board members, staff, and volunteers perform better. Many board members are inexperienced in nonprofit matters and find training enlightening. Many fundraisers have skill sets limited by their on-their-job experiences. Even fundraisers who have been around a while find additional training helpful. Volunteers need instruction on how to perform their tasks so that data collection and the donor experience are consistent between volunteers and over time.

Soft skills are crucial to successfully raising money. The number one soft skill to cultivate is your relationship-building ability. Another soft skill to advance is the art of communication. Planning skills are a must. Time management skills are also essential. Negotiating skills are critical too, especially in asking for large personal gifts.

Budget for professional development as a core operating cost, just as important as other core agency functions. Make professional development a priority. Run your numbers. Demonstrate the financial effects of choosing the continuing education investment over the cost of the alternative. Include continuing education goals in your fundraising plan. Allocate time for it, collect data on finding and obtaining it, and measure its results. Don't let a scarcity mindset get in your way. If you do need to cut costs, think seriously before cutting your professional development costs.

Points to Remember

- Investment in professional development is an investment in your nonprofit's growth, yielding high financial and human returns.

- Strengthening technical, relationship-building, communication, planning, time management, and negotiation skills will help you and your team raise more money.

- Plan for team growth. Make professional development a priority. Put aside resources for board, staff, and volunteer training.

- Incorporate raising professional development monies into your fundraising plans. Kill any scarcity mindset. If you don't think you can find the funds, you probably won't.

What's Next

So, let's review all that we've covered. You now have the tools you need to create fundraising efficiencies. You know the keys to creating an environment conducive to success. You understand how to find the money to fund your efforts. You see what data you need to collect and evaluate your efforts. You realize how to tame your fundraising fears and ask for a donation. You recognize how to build a fundraising dream team, recruit them, retain them, and develop them through training. Your next step is to actually implement what you've learned. Which requires changing things from the way they are now.

The next chapter talks about how you get your fundraising from where it currently is to where you want it to be. In other words, how you navigate the changes necessary to implement The Sustainable High ROI Fundraising System at your agency.

Chapter Fifteen

Getting from Here to There

Shaundra and her board were focused on growing their nonprofit to meet growing demand. There was a high need for the homeless services they offered in their community. They needed money to expand their shelter's capacity. But they did not want to hire another fundraiser. Shaundra needed to raise more money within the capacity of her current staff.

Shaundra knew the organizational changes she needed to make. Implementing them would be the hard part. Just how was she going to lead her agency through the changes needed to realize more net revenues?

The Goal

As we stated in **Chapter Two**, our goal is to move away from an organizational structure within which each department and the board work toward mission fulfillment but not very closely with each other, looking something like:

What you strive for is a system that looks more like:

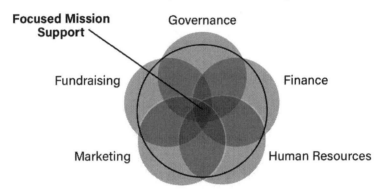

Mission and Financial Stability

Implementing The Sustainable High ROI System moves you into a system like this, where departments and their functions are integrated, the mission is supported with almost all organizational resources, and fundraising is woven into the fabric of your operations. Departments work together as one big team to reach the common goals of mission and financial sustainability.

The results of moving from the old way of operating to The Sustainable High ROI Fundraising System are remarkable. You realize immediate financial returns, enjoy board and staff working together in their respective roles, reduce your fundraising costs, and raise more money, which can then be used for mission advancement. Which attracts new donors. You raise even more money. Your mission advances again. The sustainability cycle has begun.

The question now is how you get there.

Planning for the Change

The best way to manage change is to plan for it. Yes, some change is unexpected. You cannot plan for every contingency. But you can prepare to deal with them before they happen by knowing where you are headed.

You start by visiting your strategic plan. Your strategic plan outlines your agency's path forward. If you share it and it is a working document, it keeps people all on the same page. Even during times of tumultuous change. Because your agency's mission, vision, and values stay the same. They serve as your anchor.

And, if you've done the strategic planning process correctly, your board and staff have already bought into its goals. Whatever change you're going to implement should help you reach the goals stated in the strategic plan. That way, people will see the change as necessary. It will be easier for them to understand why change is happening. They may still not like changing from the way things are, but at least they will recognize why it must be so. We talked about the importance of strategic planning in **Chapter Three**.

When you implement The Sustainable High ROI Fundraising System, you will advance change on several fronts. Some will be process interventions, like surplus budgeting and collecting data. Some will be cultural interventions, like building an environment conducive to fundraising success. Some require personal changes first, like moving from a scarcity to abundance mindset. Others focus on staff and board development, like emphasizing training and professional development.

Some changes require more planning than others. For example, changing your approach to fundraising and the resulting development plan can affect workload and cash flow, involving multiple departments. Whereas a change to emphasize donor retention over donor acquisition will probably only affect the processes of the development staff.

Generally, the smaller the scope of the intervention and the fewer people it will affect, the easier it is to make happen. Likewise, the more all-encompassing the change and the more people it will affect, the harder it is and longer it takes to catch hold.

Making the Change Happen

There are basically two approaches you can take when you decide to change the way you fundraise: the incremental approach or the radical approach. Both approaches have their own pluses and minuses. Which approach you use will depend on your situation and the level of crisis your organization is facing. And usually when it comes to fundraising, that crisis is financial in nature.

Incremental Approach

The incremental approach is defined as small changes executed over a long period of time. You transform the agency one small step at a time. It requires a long-term vision, persistence, determination, and lots of patience. You take this approach when you have time before you need to realize the total impact of the change. Leaders take this approach most often when the agency is not in a state of emergency. In regard to The Sustainable High ROI fundraising system, that is when fundraising results are adequate, but you still desire to improve them.

One of the benefits to slowly implementing change is that you have time to get people on board and prepare them for the change. For example, you have time to work with your board to do a visioning exercise, where they dare to dream of what can be and become excited about getting there. Or recruit more board members who have fundraising or marketing experience. Or you may want to provide board members with training in nonprofit life cycles and how that pertains to your organization's stage of development.

You also have time to work with your executive team, giving them the long-term goals and letting them come up with more short-term objectives and a plan for achieving them, including an implementation timeline, action plan, assignment of responsibilities, resources they need to successfully complete their work, how those resources will be obtained, and an evaluation plan. You, of course, will help them obtain the resources they require and be available to them as needed. Give them the time they need to implement their plans. We saw how to lead and develop high functioning teams in **Chapter Five**.

Using the incremental approach also means you have time to evaluate and reflect on progress. As each milestone is reached, you have time to collect performance data, analyze results, give feedback, and celebrate success. And it is important that you celebrate success. It helps increase motivation and encourages further pursuit of long-term goals.

The incremental approach also gives you time to run the numbers, determine the costs of the change, and build up dedicated reserves for the project.

The main drawback to using the incremental approach is that it can be frustrating. It takes time to see significant results. During that time, people may become weary and give up on or just lose sight of the longer-term goal. It's a lot of work on your part to keep your people excited about the change over significant periods of time and focused on the prize—the benefits.

> **Warning!**
>
> Although the incremental approach to change allows people time to prepare and adjust in stages, over time they may become weary of all the work and give up on the longer-term goal.

Radical Approach

In contrast to the incremental approach, the radical approach is quick and drastic. It immediately removes what is and replaces it with something new. You see the radical approach most often when an agency is in trouble—when a crisis threatens the organization's existence. If they want to survive, the agency must act now. There is no time to prepare everyone for the change.

In these circumstances, board members tend to have a do-or-die mindset. They may not agree on what exactly needs to be done, but they are open to strong leadership and swift action. Which gives you a lot of control over what will be done how quickly.

The staff, though, is a different story. They may be blissfully unaware of how bad things really are. As a result, they don't understand why the changes are necessary at the pace they are happening. Therefore, there is a lot of discontent. Which is passed through to the volunteers and clients. You end up in a short, bloody battle where you probably lose people. And things probably get worse before they get better.

The payoff is the organization lives on. And the upheaval doesn't last long.

The main drawback to the radical approach is that it is so disruptive. And usually not everyone survives. Either people are restructured out of a job, or they leave in frustration. There may be hard feelings.

And usually, you don't last long either. If drastic change is called for, generally you need someone new to do it. Someone who is not part of the existing system and vested in it. If you are the person coming in to make the change, chances are you are a turnaround expert whose job will be done once the change has fully taken effect.

I've led both incremental and radical change. I prefer the incremental approach, just because it is a much more pleasurable experience and there are not so many casualties. But sometimes the radical approach is necessary. And saving a nonprofit from closing its doors due to finances has its own rewards.

Managing Fundraising Change

People react to change in pretty predictable ways, as do organizations. To be an effective change agent, you need to manage those reactions to get anywhere.

Before we delve into understanding and dealing with people during times of change, you need to understand that you are dealing with people at two levels: as individuals and as a group. A group is its own entity with unique characteristics, values, and personality, just like individuals.

Large groups, like organizations, have developed systems to keep them in existence. And systems are much harder to change than individuals. There is an inertia, an energy to keep the things the way they are—the way that birthed the agency, kept it functioning, and has served it well. Systems have an inborn resistance to change.

Yet, they are moldable. Given enough time, a nonprofit will take on the characteristics of its executive director. You, as leader, exert tremendous influence over how well or poorly your agency will fare during times of change, just by you being you. As such, it is extremely important that you pay attention to your own responses to change when it occurs.

Understanding People's Reactions

When you implement The Sustainable High ROI Fundraising System, you are leading change to your revenue generating streams. Which makes it a hot topic. Money is almost always a sensitive topic.

In addition, interpreting financial statements may not be a skill board members possess. Board members may not fully understand what's going on financially. Add to that, the principles that guide fundraising are foreign to most board members. Fundraising is not a business function in the corporate world. What you end up with is a group of people who may not truly comprehend why you want to do what you want to do. They may feel a lack of control over how money is generated. And be uncomfortable with changing its incoming channels as a result.

Which is one reason why people generally do not like change. They feel out of control. Which is unpleasant to them. They don't like it. They yearn for things to return to a state of normalness, even if the previous normal was not getting them where they wanted to go. Board members may say that they want things to change, but, in my experience, more often than not they want to keep doing the same things and get different results. In other words, they don't want to change a system they know, even if it no longer works for them. The unknown is just too uncertain.

I have experienced this firsthand. For example, when I was an executive director the board and staff were very comfortable raising money through special events. But special events were not working for them. In fact, their gala was not producing enough net revenue to make the costs worth all the effort. Accounting for labor costs, the gala was breaking even, at best. Each year it brought in less and less. It was time to really look at the gala and decide whether it was worth continuing or not.

The suggestion of even questioning whether or not to have the gala or not was controversial. Several board members vehemently opposed doing away with the event, even though I had provided them with several years of net revenue trends, could demonstrate the gala's low return on investment, and outlined an alternative way to raise money (individual donations).

Clearly, the numbers showed we needed to change the way we raised money if we were to financially survive. Yet, there was still resistance to trying something new. There was this underlying fear that we would fail in our attempts to garner large individual gifts and would have to shut our doors due to lack of funding.

People don't want to experience failure. They want to feel good about the work they are performing. They want to make a valuable contribution. Failure does not get them there.

Plus, the consequences of failure may be too risky. Sometimes people would rather limp along than chance making things worse. The stakes may be too high for them. To illustrate, when the board and I finally made the decision to cancel the gala and focus on other forms of fundraising, one board member resigned from both the board and development committee, citing that she could not support the agency's downfall.

> **Food for Thought**
>
> Reactions to change are often emotional, not logical.

Of course, all these feelings may go unacknowledged. In which case, conflicts are likely to arise. Or you, as leader, become the object of their misplaced anger. Things can get really unpleasant.

Of course, a heavy fallout will probably not happen if you are making a change to your budgeting procedures. But it may happen if you are going to change your fundraising approach. Before taking on any significant change initiative, you may want to secure the services of a consultant or executive coach to help you through it.

Dealing with the Fallout

The changes you are going to make can be seen as positive—such as upgrading your technology, saving time and effort and improving productivity—or negative—such as restructuring your staff or cleaning house. The level of the reaction to the change will depend on how threatening to the status quo the change is and how much anxiety people feel about the intervening results of the change. For example, the possibility of layoffs is more threatening than changing the way grant budgets are presented. The differences in response to them will be quite different.

Try and gauge board and staff reactions to the change. Most likely, whether you implement change incrementally or suddenly, the change will be disconcerting. Which is why you need to listen to board member's and staff's concerns about the change and reassure them that their apprehension is normal. Give them coping techniques for dealing with the discomfort. Reinforce the benefits the change will bring. Paint the picture of what it will be like after the transition is over, Focus them on the end state of affairs.

If you are engineering the change, tell your people what is coming and how to prepare for it. And when the change happens, let them know what to expect—both in terms of processes and emotions. Reassure them they are up to the task. Give them encouragement along the way. When you complete the change, congratulate people on making the change happen and point out the benefits they are realizing. And help them continue in the new way of doing things.

Food for Thought

Prepare people for change. Tell them what to expect. Give them coping techniques. And focus their attention on the end benefits

Part of the change I had to implement to get our agency back on solid financial footing was immediately cut costs. Soon, it became apparent that I needed to downsize the staff. Which I did. And then had to deal with the repercussions.

The staff that were left naturally had anxiety over what would happen to them. To lessen their anxiety, I shared my fundraising plan with them, showing them how I planned to get the organization more fiscally stable. I told them things were not going to change overnight and it may get worse before it gets better. I maintained an open-door policy, letting the staff vent when they needed to. I encouraged them to take care of themselves and modeled good self-care.

As I implemented the new fundraising plan, I shared our financial progress with them. I asked them what their vision for their departments were, given more stable finances. I got them thinking about what was possible. I celebrated each milestone we reached. I helped them see how they were attaining their vision and things were getting better.

Not that these actions totally allayed their fears. They did not. It took time before they felt totally secure. But having them look to the future, see their progress in getting there, and engage in self-care helped reduce the tension.

It did get worse before it got better. But what we had after it was all over was a dedicated staff who worked hard to make the vision they created a reality. We were functioning better. The changes they made worked. The agency was healthier. It wasn't easy, but we got there.

Finding Time

Where do you find time in the day to raise the money to keep the agency afloat, much less grow it, while managing reactions to change? How do you juggle the huge task of fundraising more efficiently and directing change with managing the day-to-day operations of service delivery?

First, track how you spend your time. Make a list of your daily task and record how much time you spend on each. Then separate those tasks into three groups: emergency, important, and administrative. Next, take each task each task within the groups and rank them in order of importance. Finally, determine what tasks can be delegated and which ones you must complete in your role as executive director.

Then delegate work to others. Don't try to do this alone. It takes a team. Who does exactly what is a matter of how big your staff is and who has what strengths and weaknesses. Who can help you run your agency more efficiently? Can someone else can deal with the issue of the day while you're out building community relationships you need to move forward?

Allocate time to deal with the important but not urgent tasks, such as adopting The Sustainable High ROI Fundraising System. As an executive director of a small agency, I spent 70 percent of my week on the day-to-day operations and 30 percent of my week on building foundational relationships. What I found was three-fold: 1) when equipped with the proper tools and given opportunity my staff rose to the occasion; 2) my expectations about what I could do needed to be realistic and 3) I wasn't as indispensable as I thought. The benefits of stepping back for 30 percent of the time far exceeded what I hoped.

Taking Care of Yourself

Dealing with the fallout caused by implementing change is taxing. It can be emotionally exhausting. Although there will seem like no way to do it, you must set aside time to take care of yourself. And you must reach out for the support you need. Although working relentlessly produces great short-term gains, the long-term results are less than optimal. You get weary, the job becomes a chore, and you lose your enthusiasm for the change.

Self-care is anything you do to revitalize, escape the daily grind, forget the demands on your time, and relax. It is critical to getting through managing change. So often we put a priority on meeting other people's needs and get so caught up in making sure they are all right, that we neglect ourselves and making sure we are all right. We forget about tending to self-care.

So, schedule attendance at social events and other rejuvenating activities. Calendar time away from the office and its pressures. Indulge in personal pursuits. It's okay to occasionally have lunch with a friend instead working through it. It's okay to get your hair cut on work time if you've just worked all evening. Sometimes, we just need to give ourselves permission to take time to care for ourselves.

Taking care of yourself models the behaviors you want your staff to engage in. Employees take their cues from what their leaders do far more than what they say. The old adage 'do as I say, not as I do' doesn't work. Make sure you are engaging in the same behaviors you tell others to do. Set an example. Let them know it really is okay to put yourself first every once in a while.

Focus on caring for yourself. You and your organization will be better off for it.

Shaundra's Solution

Shaundra's first step in making the changes she knew she had to make was planning it out. She set her goal and listed everything she and her team would need to do to accomplish it. She worked backwards, marking important milestones in the journey. She figured the changes would take about two years to complete, with another year to fully integrate them into the agency's culture.

She started by initiating a strategic planning process, to get buy-in to the changes. Next, she started preparing her board, staff, and volunteers for the change. Shaundra knew there would be resistance. Not everyone would get onboard. These people would probably leave. Shaundra wanted to make sure her board and staff were prepared to deal with it. So, during board and staff meetings, Shaundra made it a point to emphasize the agreement on the need for change, the ultimate benefits they would realize after implementation was over, and the short-term costs they may pay for going ahead with it. Shaundra also brainstormed ideas for dealing with the fallout with them.

As predicted, not everyone supported the changes, especially if they were directly affected. A few members of her team expressed anger at changing the status quo. Several volunteers left.

To get through it all, Shaundra made sure she took time for herself. She needed to get away from the stress every once in a while, and she needed her staff to do the same. She knew she needed to model the behavior she wanted them to emulate.

After about two and a half years, the organization finally got to where Shaundra wanted it to be. Everyone could rest awhile, celebrate, and reap the benefits of their hard work.

Wrapping It Up

Any changes you consider making should align with the goals in your strategic plan. If you've done the strategic planning process correctly, your board and staff have already bought into its goals. Changes can include process interventions or cultural interventions, require personal change first, or focus on staff and board development. Some changes are more disruptive and require more planning than others.

There are basically two approaches you can take when you decide change to the way you fundraise is needed: the incremental approach or the radical approach. The benefits of approaching change incrementally include having time to get people on board, preparing them for the change, evaluating and reflecting on progress with them, and building up reserves for the project. The main benefit of the very disruptive radical approach is that the organization can avoid serious unwanted consequences, like closing its doors.

People generally do not like change. Common feelings around it include a lack of control and fear of failure. These feelings may go unacknowledged. As a result, conflict may arise. Or you become the object of their misplaced anger.

Which means you are taxed and may become exhausted. To counteract these negative consequences, set aside time to take care of yourself and reach out for the support you need. Give yourself permission to engage in self-care. Everyone involved will be better off for it.

Points to Remember

- Generally, the smaller the scope of the intervention and the fewer people it will affect, the easier change is to make happen. Likewise, the more all-encompassing the change and the more people it will affect, the harder it is and longer it takes to catch hold.

- Although the incremental approach gives you time to prepare for change, it can be frustrating to implement because it takes so much time to see significant results, your team may become weary and give up on the longer-term goal.

- Do not underestimate people's resistance to change.

- To help people feel comfortable with change, listen to your team's concerns, reassure them that their apprehension is normal, give them coping techniques, and reenforce the benefits of the change.

- Remember to shore up your emotional reserves by taking care of yourself.

What's Next

Engineering change, even a change perceived as positive, is not easy. The Sustainable High ROI Fundraising System provides you with the tools needed to make the changes you need to raise more money within your nonprofit's current capacity. In our next chapter, the final one, we review what those tools are and the processes critical to implementing them.

Chapter Sixteen

Moving Forward

The Sustainable High ROI Fundraising System is a roadmap that guides you through the task of realizing continuous net surpluses, giving you a sustainable stream of money to advance your mission. To implement the system, focus on creating fundraising efficiencies that achieve the highest return on investment possible. The result is a strong organizational infrastructure that builds your nonprofit's capacity and allows your agency to grow. You move from stressed to calm as board members and staff leaders work together to attract more donors and attain higher donations, community support increases, you achieve the net surpluses you need to sustainably advance your nonprofit's mission, and you meet your financial and mission goals.

The Tools You Need

The tools you need to realize continuous growth are:

- An unrelenting emphasis on mission
- An abundance mindset
- A supportive culture where board and staff are empowered to do their jobs
- A fundraising strategy that capitalizes on your nonprofit's strengths and works within the limits of your agency's capacity
- A fundraising plan that includes all factors affecting fundraising operations

- A way to provide staff with the resources they need to do their jobs
- A strong, singular identity
- Strong fundraising team recruitment and retention strategies
- The knowledge of how to navigate the change process and its consequences

The Processes You Employ

It is your mission that motivates donors to give. To be effective, your nonprofit's mission must be infused into your fundraising endeavors.

You also need to move from a scarcity mindset to a more abundant one. If you think that you will fail in fundraising because there are not enough resources to go around, you probably will. Make resources multiply. Leverage your efforts with those of other institutions.

Create an organizational environment conducive to fundraising. Help board members, development staff, and fundraising volunteers achieve their tasks.

Foster fundraising efficiencies. Work smarter, not harder. Let those efficiencies guide your fundraising strategy and resulting plan.

Develop a singular, core message that can be adapted to reach different target audiences. To make sure it resonates with your community, use key stakeholder feedback to inform the words and concepts you use in your messaging.

Don't try and pursue everybody. Your return on investment will be low. Rather, invest resources where they will have the greatest chance of producing results. Look for donors and volunteers with a connection to your cause, a propensity to give, and the capacity to give.

Recruit well. Keep good board members, development staff, and fundraising volunteers. Give them the training they need to succeed.

And manage change carefully. Even positive change can be stressful.

Evaluate Your Efforts

Regularly assess your nonprofit's fundraising strengths and gaps. Evaluation provides a systematic way to study a fundraising program and determine if it reached its goals. Pulling together and analyzing fundraising, marketing, and financial information aids in budgeting, setting and achieving goals, evaluating performance, and exploring fundraising and marketing alternatives when financial outcomes are less than desired.

Conducting regular evaluation helps you understand what worked, what didn't, and why. Develop evaluation processes, procedures, and metrics that meet development, finance, and marketing staffs' needs. Determine how well procedures were implemented, whether the process worked, what individual elements contributed to success or failure, and how well overall goals were met. Build evaluation into your fundraising operations so you have the information you need to measure your results in a timely manner. Use the numbers to benchmark fundraising performance, direct efforts to increase your return on investment, and analyze the relationship between your fundraising and marketing efforts. Let the data inform your plans.

Plan for Growth

Plan for growth and change. Engage in strategic planning. Strategic plans set direction for financial, mission, staff, and donor growth; coordinate activities between people and groups; integrate fundraising with other organizational functions; improves communication; and leverages work efforts. Finance, development, program, and marketing teams work together to create and achieve the results of their respective work plans. Define the purpose of any work teams, recruit diverse team members, and articulate a compelling vision. Let team members create an action plan. Set milestones to measure and celebrate progress.

Budget Wisely

Pay attention to the bottom line. It is net surpluses that fund your nonprofit's reserves, investment in your agency's future, and increases in organizational capacity.

If you want your agency to grow financially, budget for more than program and core operating expenses. Also include line items for operating reserves and budget contingencies.

Budget for a surplus. To ensure a surplus, budget your fundraising expenses 5 percent higher and revenues 5 percent lower than you think they will be. Account for time and labor in your cost analyses. If you must cut costs, cut them in a way that will bring you the most long-term benefit.

Allocate resources wisely. Focus on improving your donor retention rate. Reduce your opportunity costs. Compare the returns on investment of your fundraising options. Plan activities that bring in the most amount of money using the least amount of resources. Increase revenues while containing costs. Change your revenue mix if you have to.

Don't cut anything that yields a good return on investment. When you do realize positive net income, set aside some of the excess for operating reserves, capacity building, and investing in long-term assets. Prepare for staff growth and its resulting costs.

And build wealth. Invest in long-term revenue-generating assets. Pay attention to the balance sheet just as much as the profit and loss statement.

Establish Your Team

Board, staff, and volunteers all have a role in fundraising. The board governs while staff and volunteers facilitate operations. It is important that all your team members are of good character, have discretion, and can keep confidentialities. All three constituencies should be screened, interviewed, and assessed for fit before they are asked to become part of the agency. They should also be aware of the state of your nonprofit, lines of information, their roles, and the commitments they are making.

Your Board

The board's job is to strategically allocate resources and monitor their acquisition. They focus on strategy and provide an environment that supports the executive director and staff in implementing those strategies. To fill board vacancies, have board members create a matrix that outlines the makeup of their ideal board. Train them to reach out to candidates based where the holes are. Create a recruitment packet that helps prospective board members understand your agency, their role as a board member, and the commitments involved in serving. Be open with prospects, sharing both the good and the not so good about your nonprofit. When they are asked to serve, reiterate expectations.

Then provide a good board experience. Have new members meet with the president. Have the president assign them a mentor and get them involved right away. Provide them with training. Offer work that focuses on mission fulfillment strategies, not operations. Facilitate a mid-year check-in to see how it's going. Help your board chair facilitate regular board evaluations. Continuously express your gratitude for their service.

Engage your board so they willingly fundraise. Help board members plan for the future. Address long-term objectives during board meetings. Teach your board how to ask strategic fundraising questions. Build strong, personal relationships with board members.

Your Staff

As you add development staff, hire enlightened generalists rather the traditional fundraising specialists. Structure job functions around donors' needs, not giving channels. To afford experienced development professionals, considering hiring them part-time, and present exciting opportunities to shape the future. Highlight the position's contribution to mission fulfillment, working partnership with the executive director, flexible work schedule, continuing education opportunities, and diversity, equity, inclusion, and access initiatives. Look for relationship-building, analytical, problem-solving, and conflict resolution skills; fundraising expertise and performance; their priorities, values, sense of personal responsibility; and their adherence to ethical standards during the job interview. When you present the offer, have them sign a confidentiality agreement and non-compete clause.

Equip your fundraising staff with the tools necessary to meet their financial goals. Develop their skills. Encourage diversity of thought. Budget for professional development. Give team leaders discretion over the resources they need to accomplish their goals. Allow autonomy but clearly define their scope of authority. Regularly review their progress. Work with your development team to make fundraising happen. Acknowledge their contributions to regularly.

Provide staff with direction, delineate lines of communication, and discuss your working relationship with them. Delineate expectations up front. Create fundraising goals that are attainable and reasonable for your nonprofit. Apprise your development director of internal and external changes. Build a culture of philanthropy with them. Appreciate a job well done. And show them how they can continue to develop in their position.

Your Volunteers

Fundraising volunteers freely give their time and talent, moderating workload and increasing your resource base. Look for fundraising volunteers who have an interest in your mission, a connection to your agency, and the time to give to volunteering. Interview potential volunteers to assess their skills, interests, time availability, and training needs. Help volunteers say "yes" by giving them amazing opportunities to make a difference.

Give them job descriptions, orientation, training, and ongoing supervision. Discuss your expectations up front. Offer constructive feedback on their performance. Provide them with the tools they need to successfully complete their tasks. Constantly thank them for their service. Publicly reward them. Make the volunteer experience as pleasing and satisfying as possible.

Lead Your Team Forward

Employ a strengths-based approach. Focus on your nonprofit's and team's assets. Staff, board, and volunteers are much more likely to stick around if the work environment is cheerful, appreciative, and accepting. Create a strengths-based culture internally so you have board, staff and volunteer mission ambassadors communicating positive message to the community. Discern and convey your agency's uniqueness. Inspire staff to convey organizational advantages to others. Ensure a robust corporate image by auditing your internal documents for consistency and revising them as necessary.

Be appreciative. Communicate gratefulness. Maintain a can-do-it attitude. Form relationships with optimistic people. Maintain a positive attitude, Reward positivity in others. Provide encouraging feedback during performance reviews. Express appreciation for a job well done.

Excite Your Community

Enthuse your community about your cause. Describe your needs as the community defines them so your mission is seen as relevant by them. Start fashioning messages that the community can relate to by getting a baseline of their perceptions. Have your team set goals based on this information. Craft messages that let potential supporters know their investment in your agency is worth it. Incorporate words and concepts that excite them in your communications. You get those words and concepts from key stakeholder feedback.

When you reach out to your community, expend resources where they are most likely to produce results. Cultivate specific donor groups, those with the propensity and capability to give. Target community members who have a profile similar to your most valuable donors. Also mine your organization's connections, hold cultivation events, research 990s, and comb through NOFAs. Generate more leads by offering an incentive on your website that encourages visitors to leave their names and email addresses. Set up a series of welcome emails to send to new donors to thank them, engage them, and improve their retention.

If you've positioned your nonprofit as poor and weak, you will not raise as much money as you could otherwise. To change the community's perception of your agency, focus on your organizational assets, create a strong brand and brand experience, make messaging consistent throughout all operational documents, differentiate your nonprofit, and emphasize mission when talking about money.

Ask for the Money You Need

The purpose of your first interaction with a potential donor is to connect, find information, and get a better understanding of each other. Build a relationship before you ask for money.

If you're anxious when the time comes to ask for money, focus on the impact a donation would make and talk about the difference your nonprofit makes in the community. View your nervousness as your mind's way of revving you up for the situation. See the donor as human on equal footing with you. If you fear the worst, ask yourself how likely your dreaded outcome is. Know the worst that can happen is they say "no" and you're no worse off than you were before.

Prepare yourself for the interaction. Do your research. Practice your pitch beforehand. De-stress by listening to music, taking a walk, or journaling. Practice deep breathing. Tense and relax the muscles in your body. Picture yourself calm. Watch your body posture. Sit up straight, speak slowly, and maintain eye contact. Ask questions. Listen more than you speak. And be yourself.

When you ask, ask the donor to join you on the road to success. Limit your request to one thing—making a donation of x amount. Be brief and get down to the point. Ask for a specific amount. And then stop talking. Let them be the first to break the silence.

Tell them how their donations were used in terms of mission fulfillment in the community, not on the organization. Thank donors regularly and often. No one has ever been offended by being authentically thanked too much. If you want another donation, keep them engaged. Ensure your communications go both ways. Acknowledge and express gratitude for every donation.

Navigate Change Carefully

If you want different results, you must do things differently. You must introduce change. Any changes you make should align with the goals in your strategic plan. Changes range in scope from implementing a new process to shaping a new culture. They may require personal change first. They can focus on board or staff development.

Some changes are more disruptive and require more planning than others. If you are considering a change, even if it is a positive change that will increase net income, gather evidence supporting it and address people's fears of it. Run the numbers so they have objective data on which to make decisions. Calm them so they can hear you. Then let them discover the facts. Allow them to come to their own conclusions. Invest them in their decisions.

The two approaches you can take to change are the incremental approach and the radical approach. Instituting change incrementally allows time to get people on board and prepared for the change. You also have time to evaluate and reflect on progress with them. And build up reserves for the project. Although the incremental approach gives you time, it can be frustrating to implement because it takes so long to see significant results. As a result, your team may become weary and give up.

The radical approach is more disruptive. Its main benefit is that the organization avoids even more of the unwanted consequences brought through the passage of time. Generally, the smaller the scope of the change, the easier it is to make happen. Likewise, the more all-encompassing the change is, the harder it is to implement.

Do not underestimate the resistance to change. People generally do not like change. Common feelings around it include a lack of control and fear of failure, sometimes provoking conflict and anger. Which means you may become overly taxed and exhausted.

To counteract these negative consequences, set aside time to take care of yourself, listen to your team's concerns, reassure them that their apprehension is normal, and reinforce the benefits of the change. In addition, give yourself permission to engage in self-care. Model healthy coping techniques, especially if you want people to emulate you. You and your followers will be better off if everyone has time rejuvenate.

The Benefits You Reap

Implementing The Sustainable High ROI Fundraising System is not for the faint of heart. It takes work to effect fundraising change and realize positive results. But the benefits are worth it. By applying the system's principles, you will realize immediate ways to raise more money, recruit new donors, see increasingly larger donations, reduce your overall fundraising costs, and enjoy ongoing net surpluses.

As you raise awareness of your nonprofit in the community, you attract more advocates to your cause. These advocates are then galvanized to spread the word about your agency. As people more people learn and become excited about your mission, they can be asked to financially support your cause. As they respond, you realize increased financial support. Which you can then pour back into your mission. And meeting more mission encourages more community support. Which results in more donations.

Your agency becomes sustainable. You know that your nonprofit will improve the human condition long into the future. You have accomplished what you set out to do when you became an executive director.

Appendix A

Essential Fundraising Evaluation Metrics

Fundraising Net Income

Net income is the total amount of donations your nonprofit realized minus fundraising expenses over a specific reporting period. Trends in fundraising net revenue indicate your nonprofit's ability to realize a surplus.

$$\text{Fundraising Revenues} - \text{Fundraising Costs}$$

Average Gift Per Donor

The average gift per donor is calculated by dividing the amount of donations received by the total number of donors that gave during the same period.

$$\frac{\text{Total Amount of Donations Received}}{\text{Total Number of Donors}}$$

Average Donor Lifespan

Average donor lifespan tells you how long your average donor gives to your organization. It is calculated by dividing the number of years your agency has been receiving donations by the number of donors over the same time period.

$$\frac{\text{Number of Years You Have Been Receiving Donations}}{\text{Total Number of Donors}}$$

Average Donor Frequency

The average donor frequency tells you how often your average donor bestows a gift to your organization. You calculate average donor frequency by dividing in total number of donations by the total number of donors during the same time period.

$$\frac{\text{Total Number of Donations}}{\text{Total Number of Donors}}$$

Cost to Raise One Dollar

To calculate your costs to raise a dollar, divide your fundraising expenses by your fundraising revenues.

$$\frac{\text{Fundraising Expenses}}{\text{Fundraising Revenues}}$$

Average Cost Per Donor

The average cost per donor is calculated by dividing the total costs of your fundraising program by the total number of donors that gave during the same period.

$$\frac{\text{Total Fundraising Program Costs}}{\text{Total Number of Donors}}$$

Donor Acquisition Rate

Your donor acquisition rate tells you the rate of growth of your donor base. Your donor acquisition rate is calculated by dividing the difference between the number of donors this year minus the number of donors last year divided by the number of donors last year.

$$\frac{(\text{Total Number of Donors This Year} - \text{Total Number of Donors Last Year})}{\text{Total Number of Donors Last Year}}$$

Donor Retention Rate

Your donor retention rate tells you the percentage of total donors that made a second gift. Your donor retention rate is calculated by dividing the total number of repeat donors this year by the total number of donors last year.

$$\frac{\text{Number of Repeat Donors This Year}}{\text{Total Number of Donors Last Year}}$$

Donor Acquisition Cost

To calculate your cost to acquire a donor, divide the expenses used to recruit new donors by the number of new donors.

$$\frac{\text{New Donor Recruitment Costs}}{\text{Total Number of Donors This Year}}$$

Donor Retention Cost

To calculate the costs of retaining a donor, divide recurring fundraising expenses by the number of recurring donors.

$$\frac{\text{Recurring Fundraising Expenses}}{\text{Number of Recurring Donors}}$$

Return on Fundraising Investment

Return on fundraising investment tells you how well your resources are financially performing. The ratio expresses what percentage of your gross revenues are devoted to costs. To calculate return on fundraising investment, divide fundraising net income by fundraising expenses.

$$\frac{\text{Total Fundraising Revenues} - \text{Total Fundraising Expenses}}{\text{Total Fundraising Expenses}}$$

Donor Lifetime Value

Your donor lifetime value is an estimate of the total amount of donations you can expect from a donor from first gift to last gift. Donor lifetime value is calculated by multiplying average donor lifespan, average gift per donor, and average donor frequency together.

Average donor lifespan x average gift per donor x average donor frequency

Appendix B

Sample Key Stakeholder Interview Questions

To get a complete view of what the whole community knows and thinks about your agency, ask you your constituencies these questions:

1. Tell me a little about what you know of [nonprofit].

2. When you think of [nonprofit], what is the first thing you think of?

3. What do you think the most important thing [nonprofit] does is?

4. What appeals most to you about [nonprofit]?

5. How did you first hear about [nonprofit]?

6. Tell me a little about your involvement with [nonprofit].

7. Would you or are you considering increasing your support through volunteering or donating to [nonprofit]?

8. Why or why not?

9. What would move you to be more engaged with [nonprofit]?

10. What one piece of advice would you give to [nonprofit] so that it is better able to advance its mission?

Appendix C

Sample Development Committee Job Description

Purpose: The development committee serves as the bridge between the governance activities of the board and the operational activities of the staff. Its purpose is to ensure revenue generation and lead board member participation in fundraising.

Responsibilities:

- Work with appropriate staff to develop a long-range and short-range development plan.

- Plan and oversee all fundraising efforts of the organization and appoint committee members to oversee fundraising activities.

- Assure full board participation in all campaigns and projects.

- Be familiar with the theory and techniques of development programs.

- Advocate to the full board the importance of fundraising to meeting the nonprofit's mission.

- Encourage the participation of all board members in fundraising activities and programs.

- Attend the agency's fundraising activities.

- Encourage board members' attendance at important agency happenings.

- Develop a plan to increase community involvement with the organization.

Time commitment: Monthly 90-minute meeting

Sample Board Member Candidate Interview Questions

Before asking people to serve on your board, interview them and assess their suitability for leadership.

- Why are you interested in our organization?
- What do you know about us?
- What experience do you have related to our mission?
- What connections/contacts can you contribute?
- How much time can you contribute?
- What other resources can you contribute?
- What qualities make a good board member?
- What personal qualities can you bring to the board?
- What do you expect from our organization?
- What factors in your life might inhibit your ability to serve?
- How do you feel about performance evaluations?
- Will you feel comfortable conducting a self-evaluation?
- What motivates you as an individual?
- What role do you think you would play on the board?

- Would you be willing to attend a lunch with the executive director in which the goal was to ask for money?

- What do you know about the field?

- Do you have any questions for us?

Appendix E

Sample Fundraising Staff Candidate Interview Questions

During job interviews with fundraising candidates, look for relationship-building, analytical, problem-solving, and conflict resolution skills; fundraising knowledge; and financial prowess. Explore their priorities, values, sense of personal responsibility, and adherence to ethical standards. Ask questions like:

1. Tell me about yourself.

2. What is your greatest strength?

3. What is your biggest weakness?

4. Why do you want this job?

5. How has your experience prepared you for this role?

6. What makes you uniquely qualified for this job?

7. How do you define fundraising success?

8. How much money do you raise in a typical year? Is that net or gross revenues?

9. What kind of fundraising have you done in the past and how successful were you?

10. What professional accomplishment are you most proud of?

11. Tell me about a time you overcame a fundraising challenge.

12. Tell me about a time you failed to meet your financial goals.

13. Tell me why you think you failed to reach your financial goals.

14. What would you do differently to reach your financial goals today?

15. Tell me about a time you failed to meet your donor relationship goal.

16. Tell me why you think you failed to save or develop the relationship.

17. What would you do differently to keep the donor or move the donor up the ladder today?

18. Tell me about how you work with board members.

19. Tell me about a time you worked with a difficult board member.

20. Tell me about a time when you worked with a difficult donor.

21. Tell me about a time you were recognized by your executive director for your work.

22. Tell me about a time you worked hard, achieved your goal, and someone else got the credit.

23. Tell me about an ethical dilemma you had and how you handled it.

24. What do you hope this job has that your last one didn't?

25. What are your career goals?

26. If you were hired, what might make you leave?

27. Do you have anything else to tell me?

28. Do you have any questions for me?

Sample Volunteer Candidate Interview Questions

Questions to ask people interested in volunteering for your nonprofit include:

1. What are your interests?

2. What skills do you bring with you?

3. What skills do you hope to acquire?

4. What else do you hope to gain from your volunteer experience?

5. How does this commitment fit in with all your other commitments?

6. How much time do you have?

7. How much flexibility do you want?

8. Do you want to work alone or in a group?

9. What kind of assignment to you want—ongoing, short-term, long-term, or one-time?

10. How long do want the assignment to be?

Index

Other Books by Joanne Oppelt

https://amzn.to/3rIJhp8

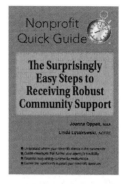

https://amzn.to/3hyJk1q

https://amzn.to/3nYdzjP

https://amzn.to/3myxI1F

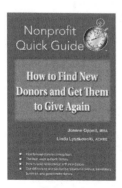

https://amzn.to/2MTcbxZ

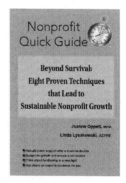

https://amzn.to/3AR9ap4

https://amzn.to/347DugS

https://amzn.to/38gASyu

https://amzn.to/2H2Q0FX

https://amzn.to/2NgdFFO

https://amzn.to/2NgdFFO

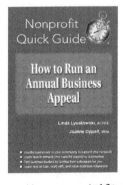

https://amzn.to/3lf5ciG

https://amzn.to/32c9eB2

https://amzn.to/2JXQjmz

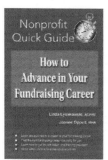

https://amzn.to/2Sgx1ZV

https://amzn.to/38AjdzJ

https://amzn.to/3cLv1BL

https://amzn.to/31lJ0e1

https://amzn.to/3ker0tI

JoanneOppelt

Seven Simple Strategies to Creating a Wildly Successful Fundraising Program

13 Ten to Twenty-Minute Classes | Private Coaching | Lifetime Access

Create a wildly successful program that generates tremendous fundraising revenues at the least amount of cost.

https://www.joanneoppeltcourses.com/seven-simple-strategies-course-and-coaching-info

How to Answer the Eight Questions Every Grant Review Committee Asks

11 Ten to Twenty-Minute Classes | Private Coaching | Lifetime Access

Get the insight and skills you need to write compelling proposals that get funded, including crafting grant budgets.

https://www.joanneoppeltcourses.com/eight-questions-course-and-coaching-info

JoanneOppelt

Best-Kept Secrets to Engaging and Retaining Business Donors

14 Ten to Twenty-Minute Online Classes | Private Coaching | Lifetime Access

Penetrate your business community, attract business donors, and get big corporate donations.

https://www.joanneoppeltcourses.com/best-kept-secrets-course-and-coaching-info

About Joanne Oppelt Consulting, LLC

Joanne Oppelt Consulting is a national fundraising firm offering books, online trainings, and in-person fundraising counsel to nonprofits seeking to advance their missions and grow their finances.

Mission

Joanne Oppelt Consulting's mission is to help deeply mission-oriented nonprofits build sustainable revenue streams.

Vision

I envision a world where highly mission-driven organizations are equipped with the tools and infrastructure necessary to financially sustain themselves.

Values

- Authenticity in all my professional dealings
- Brutal honesty with myself and my clients, fully disclosing my personal and business approach and interests
- Two-way ethical transactions in all my business partnerships
- Fairness in pricing and workload when taking on new clients
- Partnerships with ethical, top-notch practitioners to provide needed services outside my areas of expertise
- Engagement in non-political, non-sectarian causes

https://www.joanneoppeltcourses.com

Made in the USA
Columbia, SC
10 April 2024

34064518R00154